Fences, Gates & Walls
How To Design And Build

by S. Chamberlin and J. Pollock

HPBooks

Acknowledgments

Annette Schooler, Santa Cruz, CA
Barbara Iris, Designer, Santa Cruz, CA
Barbara Parrish, Santa Cruz, CA
Centennial Home Improvement Center, Tucson, AZ
Dalton Masonry, Maryville, TN
David A. Burgess, Brick Institute of America, McLean, VA
Dr. and Mrs. Ambrose Cowden, Santa Cruz, CA
Dr. Gordon C. Hall, San Antonio, TX
Dr. William and Christine Cress, Troy, MI
Fred Ray, Palo Alto, CA
George Landis, Marysville, CA
Gordan Knapp, Masonry Institute of America, Palo Alto, CA
Harry Tsugawa, Landscape Architect, Santa Cruz, CA
Historic New Orleans Collection, New Orleans, LA
Joanne and Gordon Schontzler, Santa Cruz, CA
Katherine Stedman, Landscape Architect, Palo Alto, CA
Lloyd and Linda Byars, Atlanta, GA
Longue Vue Gardens, New Orleans, LA
Louise Savette, Santa Monica, CA
Marjorie Follmer, Santa Cruz, CA
M. A. Jarvis, Yuba City, CA
Mr. and Mrs. Edwin Morgan, Carmel, CA
Mr. and Mrs. K. Van Strumm, Hillsborough, CA
Mr. and Mrs. Worth Brown, Santa Cruz, CA
Mrs. Elizabeth Stringer, Santa Cruz, CA
Mrs. James Lowe, San Francisco, CA
Napa Builders Supply Co., Napa, CA
Paula Fishman, Santa Monica, CA
Pittsburgh Corning Corporation, Pittsburgh, PA
Rebecca Niven, Santa Cruz, CA
Richard Vacha, Designer, Santa Cruz, CA
Robert and Edy Rittenhouse, Santa Cruz, CA
Robert Hagopian, Santa Cruz, CA
Robert Mondavi Winery, Oakville, CA
Roy Rydell, Landscape Architect, Santa Cruz, CA
St. George Restaurant, St. Helena, CA
Sydney Temple, Carmel, CA
Terry Watson, Santa Cruz, CA
The Cloisters, New York, NY
Thomas D. Church, Landscape Architect, San Francisco, CA
Tri-City Fence Co., Vallejo, CA
Vern Bowie, Designer, Santa Cruz, CA
Well-Sweep Herb Farm, Port Murray, NJ

About The Authors

Susan Chamberlin is a Landscape Architect in Berkeley, Calif. Chamberlin specializes in designing functional and attractive landscapes. She received her degree in landscape architecture from the University of California.

Janet Pollock is a practicing Landscape Architect in Santa Cruz, California. Pollock's work focuses on detailed design in residential landscapes as well as community and commericial projects.

About The Illustrator

Roy Jones is a professional designer and illustrator living in southern California. Jones has provided detailed illustrations for eight HPBooks. His illustrations have appeared in national magazines, books and calendars.

Cover photography by Richard Fish. Fence design by Galper/Baldon and Associates, Landscape Architects, Venice, California.

Contents

HPBooks®

Executive Editor: Rick Bailey
Editorial Director: Randy Summerlin
Editors: Larry E. Wood and Jim Barrett
Art Director: Don Burton
Book Design: Leslie Sinclair
Typography: Cindy Coatsworth and Michelle Claridge

For Horticultural Publishing Inc.

Executive Producer: Richard M. Ray
Production Editor: Kathleen S. Parker
Coordinating Editor: Michael MacCaskey
Associate Editor: Lance Walheim
Photographer: Michael Landis
Photographer: William C. Aplin
Photographic Assistant: Richard B. Ray
Illustrator: Roy Jones

Published by HPBooks®, P.O. Box 5367, Tucson, AZ 85703
602/888-2150

ISBN: 0-89586-189-5
Library of Congress Catalog Card Number: 82-84557
©1983 Fisher Publishing Inc.
Printed in U.S.A.

1

SHAPING YOUR OUTDOOR ENVIRONMENT

Barbed wire changed the western lands from wide-open range to controlled grazing areas.

Left: The Great Wall of China is 1,500 miles long. It is 15 to 30 feet tall and 12 to 20 feet wide.

Fences, gates and walls have served mankind throughout history. The first fence or wall was probably a barrier of rocks and sticks piled in front of a cave. This crude fence helped protect prehistoric man from hungry animals.

One of the most famous walls in the world is the Great Wall of China. It was built in the third century B.C. to keep invaders out of China. The wall is 1,500 miles long and is 15 to 30 feet tall and 12 to 20 feet wide.

The famous and infamous barbed wire fence of the American West was invented and patented by Joe F. Glidden in 1874. Barbed wire is used by farmers and cattlemen to establish boundaries and keep livestock contained. Barbed wire changed the livestock industry forever.

This chapter discusses important points to consider when planning a fence, gate or wall. A collection of eye-catching fence, gate and wall designs is presented as idea-starters.

The following three chapters discuss the basic components and techniques for building fences, gates and walls. Directions for constructing these fundamental forms are detailed with step-by-step instructions. Several classic designs are presented in each chapter. Beginners can build these designs as shown. Experienced or imaginative builders can add modifications to basic designs. To make the construction process easy to understand, start simple and elaborate on details later.

The final chapter is a primer. The primer provides basic information on everything related to building fences, gates and walls—from adobe to hardware and mortar to veneer brick. Turn to the primer for help as questions arise. The primer is arranged in alphabetical order for easy reference.

Climbing roses soften this painted concrete-block wall. Wall is constructed of square blocks in running-bond pattern. Pilaster blocks form *pilasters,* or columns, for reinforcement. Control joints are located at each point where the wall steps down the slope.

Fences, gates and walls serve many purposes. They are used for practical and decorative functions in gardens and yards. They can change the look of outdoor spaces, define boundaries, discourage intruders and ensure privacy. They perform decorative functions, providing attractive backgrounds for flowers and shrubs and serving as visual points of interest in designed landscapes.

This book contains many ideas for using fences, gates and walls. Use your imagination to create other uses as you look through these pages.

Deciding What To Build

There are many points to consider when deciding to build a fence or a wall. The first and most important point is the need or purpose of the structure. Why do you need a fence or wall? After you've determined what the need is, you can decide whether to build a fence or wall. The next step is to decide on architectural style or design and type of materials to use.

Then integrate the design in the landscape and estimate construction costs.

PRACTICAL PURPOSES OF FENCES AND WALLS

Here are some of the most common practical purposes of fences and walls.

Boundary Markers—Fences and walls are used to establish property lines and visual boundary markers. They help define specific areas of use in a garden: recreation, vegetable gardens, flower gardens, relaxation and storage.

Privacy And Views—Fences, gates and walls provide privacy. They block views and control access from outside into the yard or garden. Fences and walls can screen or define and frame views. Shutters placed over openings in a fence can open or close a view or admit light and air. Small screens can conceal air-conditioning units and refuse containers.

Tall fences and walls can deter unwelcome visitors or intruders. Gates can establish privacy by presenting a formidable barrier to entry or by giving an uninviting impression.

Fence rails fit into slots in these stone columns. Columns are made of concrete block covered with stone veneer.

Protection—There are many different types of barrier fences and walls. Barriers are designed to keep people or animals in or out of a specific area. Barrier fences and walls are usually over 6 feet tall. They can have protective elements added. Livestock fences are normally made from posts and barbed wire. Barbed wire is used on top of chain-link fences or walls. Fences can be electrified to discourage intruders or keep livestock inside. Walls can have metal spikes or wrought-iron work placed on top to discourage intruders.

Tall walls or solid-board fences are effective barriers. The psychological effect of solid structures may sometimes be more effective at stopping intruders than taller, open types of fencing that allow a view of the interior.

Fences and walls keep people away from swimming pools or other potential hazards. In rural areas, wire fences are commonly used to contain livestock and pets.

The well-designed metal fence at right keeps small children and uninvited guests from entering the swimming pool area. The fence's open structure allows cooling breezes and warm sunlight to enter the surrounding deck.

Livestock fencing, topped by barbed wire, keeps animals confined in designated areas. This fence material is strong and flexible.

Chain-link fencing, topped by barbed wire, discourages intruders from entering restricted areas. Chain-link fencing is used extensively in commercial and residential applications.

Environment Control—Fences, walls and screens alter *microclimates* in gardens, serving as windbreaks or creating shade in sunny locations. Microclimates are small areas in a landscape that have different climatic conditions. These small, localized climates are influenced by sunlight, wind, shade, moisture and other factors described below.

Temperatures Are Altered by carefully planning the type of structure and location in the landscape. Masonry walls are effective *heat exchangers* or heat reservoirs on the side facing the sun. Heat exchangers transfer heat energy from a warm medium to a cooler one. Walls absorb the sun's heat and store heat for a limited time. As air outside the wall becomes cooler, the heat stored in the wall radiates out to warm the area.

Living fences of plants such as screens or hedges can add moisture to the air through *transpiration*. Transpiration is the process of giving off water through the surface of leaves and other parts of plants.

Airflow can be directed by placement of fences, walls and hedges.

Light Is Directed by fences and walls. Dark indoor rooms can be brightened. Light-color walls and fence surfaces can be placed to bounce sunlight into dark, interior rooms. Other walls or fences can be placed to provide shade.

Noise Is Controlled by placing fences and walls at strategic locations around a yard. Walls are most effective at muting and deflecting noise. A tall, thick, solid structure works best. Fences mute noise slightly. Fences and walls do have a significant effect on what you think you hear by blocking the visual source of noise.

Painted wall is built in stack-bond pattern. Blocks are turned so open cells admit light and air. Wood cap is anchored to top course of blocks.

Lattice creates interesting shadow patterns and admits light into a dark corner of deck. Fenceposts support a bench and pots of flowers.

Structural Uses—Fences and walls are used for structural support and independent structures in and around gardens. Fences can be designed as built-in storage areas or to support espaliers. Masonry or timber retaining walls can terrace slopes and prevent movement of soil on hillsides. Walls can be designed to confine private courtyards. See page 24 for more information on courtyards.

Low wall is covered with stucco. The wall sculpturally defines the terrace edge, linking it to the wall and landscape. Wide wall top provides seating area.

Glass is used to enclose this space and shelter an outdoor-living area without blocking views or light.

Golden Delicious apple trees espaliered on post-and-wire fence resemble a hedge and provide a bountiful harvest. This espalier needs no more space than many fences. For more on espaliers, see the HP book, *Hedges, Screens and Espaliers.*

Ornate metal gates at the entrance to this home provide visitors with an inviting view of the yard. Vertical wood screens and stucco wall add warmth to the entrance. Blue tile roof over the entry adds color and shelter.

Entrances—The obvious function of gates is to control access, but gates can do much more. A sense of welcome is created by an open gate that permits outsiders to catch a glimpse inside. In Spain and the southern United States, an open gate is a tacit invitation for visitors to enter and enjoy the cool of the garden.

Gates that blend with fencing or solid, imposing gates signal that the people inside value privacy.

Designing gates for fences or walls includes more than ornamental detailing. The gate's location in the fence or wall, adjacent plantings and other structures must be considered. This lets you create an integrated gateway between two spaces.

The size and strength of gates is important. Gates must be wide for easy entrance of people or automobiles if the gate is across a driveway. The wider the gate, the stronger it must be to prevent sagging.

Graceful lattice gate contrasts with the sturdy brick wall. Gate provides an attractive transition from one garden area to another.

Smooth-surface stucco wall and wrought-iron gate enclose typical New Orleans courtyard. Design is a regional style common in the South. The gate is contemporary, but blends well with the wall and environment.

Zig-zag fence of rustic split rails is typical type of pioneer fencing.

THINK ABOUT ESTHETICS

A second major consideration in designing fences, gates or walls is how they look in the environment. It may be important to integrate fences, gates or walls into the landscape and regional character of the neighborhood. They can also reflect the architectural style of the home and community.

Before choosing a design to build, look at the types and styles of fences, gates and walls in the surrounding community. Study the materials they are made from—wood, stone, brick or chain-link fencing—to determine the suitability for your yard.

Other considerations include style treatments and painted colors or natural finishes. Rustic or sophisticated treatments are usually derived from regional traditions. These styles help give an area a sense of history or regionality. You may discover the best kind of boundary or barrier fencing for your property is a mass planting of thorny rambler roses.

Don't hesitate to create your own style or use selected historic elements from your area. Original elements can add a unique appearance to ordinary structures.

The scale of your property is an important consideration when choosing a fence or wall design. A 10-foot-high block wall might look out of place around a small suburban home lot. A short picket fence may not suit the scale of a lavish 20-acre estate.

Legal Requirements—The construction of fences and walls is usually regulated by local *building codes*. Building codes may restrict the height, type of structure, materials and location on your property. Check local building regulations before planning and building any fence, gate or wall.

White-painted stucco is troweled over new concrete-block wall. Rough, textured surface is a traditional finish. Old adobe or brick walls need special surface preparation to ensure stucco will adhere to basic structure.

Gate with Z-frame brace prevents sagging by supporting the frame. Brace from lower hinge side to upper latch side counteracts sag. Tall, curved pickets were cut with a portable electric sabre saw.

Integrated Plantings

Fences, gates and walls that are integrated into planted landscapes produce a natural look. Shrubs and hedges can disguise a fence, soften the look of a wall or conceal barbed wire. Plants can provide privacy and limited noise control. Fences and walls can support espaliers or vines, or transform a steep slope into a terraced garden. Plants add color and form to the garden and can provide a bountiful harvest of edible fruits and herbs.

Hedges are living fences. They usually cost less than wooden or metal counterparts. Hedges and gates in combination are an inexpensive substitute for fences, gates and walls. To deter intruders, plant thorny species 1 to 2 feet apart, or hide a barbed-wire or metal-security fence within a living wall of foliage.

Local ordinances often restrict the height of fences or walls or establish setbacks from property lines. Hedges are seldom regulated by building codes. You can grow a high hedge to extend the height of a low fence for privacy.

Hedges can also be grown in portable containers to provide temporary screening. The planted containers can be moved wherever needed. Hedges make good privacy screens on roof gardens. They can divide large expanses of paving into attractive smaller areas. Narrow boxes can be set on top of low walls to extend privacy screening above eye level.

Vines can dress up and disguise chain-link or wire fencing. The appearance is much the same as a hedge, but the width required is little more than for the fence. Vines can be trained and clipped to conceal a gate in a fence. Large expanses of fences and walls can be made less harsh looking with vines. Train the vines in intricate patterns to decorate plain surfaces.

Be selective in choosing plants. Some vines grow rapidly and are hard to control. Fast-growing vines require

Broken concrete is an inexpensive material for walls. Concrete gives a rustic stone look. Use a wall 16 inches high for seating and to make raised planting beds for annuals, perennials and herbs.

High wood fence blocks view between yard and busy street. Related plantings of trees and shrubs provide buffer between yard and busy street.

Chain-link fence covered with vines makes an attractive boundary fence. View is partially concealed without being blocked.

Low wood wall combined with living wall of English laurel is effective privacy screen between street and the garden.

This rustic wall is concrete block covered with stucco. Natural gray color of stucco harmonizes with cap of used brick. Plantings add appeal to large expanse of wall.

Wood arbor and hawthorn plantings pruned as an aerial hedge frame a view of this small formal garden.

Verrier-palmette espalier softens brick wall. Pears will grow well in reflected heat from wall.

Pyracantha grown against this wall demonstrates formal growth patterns of espalier training.

Low hedge of holly softens lines of low stone wall around garden fountain. Related plantings at fountain's base make this an inviting resting area.

Wire on a weathered-wood frame makes an attractive and economical fence. Fence is used to enclose a utility yard. Hedge behind fence screens view of wood pile.

continuous maintenance to prevent them from damaging fences or walls.

Espalier is an ancient art. Espalier is a method of training plants to grow flat against a wall or framework in a formal pattern. Espalier plants are vinelike, but the growth direction is carefully controlled. Espaliers grown on post-and-wire fences require little space. Espalier fruit plants improve the privacy value of inexpensive fences and produce large quantities of fruit.

In colder climates, dwarf apple or pear trees are planted as espaliers. In subtropical climates, lemons, tangerines and oranges are espaliered to provide year-round greenery.

Fruit espaliers are traditionally trained against walls or on supportive fences. Walls are favored because the heat from sunlight is stored in the masonry. The warm wall produces a favorable microclimate for ripening fruit.

A support framework positioned 6 inches away from wall surfaces prevents radiated heat from overheating or cooking foliage and fruit. Heat-loving varieties of fruit may be trained directly on walls.

Lattice fences are quickly covered by vines. Lattice fences are the perfect support for espaliers. Lattice and solid-wood fences store less heat than masonry walls. Espaliers can be tied directly to wood without damage.

Hawthorn grown on an *arbor,* a wooden support structure, can be pruned into an aerial hedge. The hedge provides a ceiling for the outdoor room shown in the top photograph on page 16. The hedge frames a view of flower and herb beds.

In the same photograph, hedge in background conceals a potting shed and path to the guest house. The path is similar to a hallway. The path is screened from nearby neighbors by a second arbor and grapestake fencing. The fence steps down along the slope.

The photograph at left shows an attractive lot boundary fencing. The fence is made from economical welded-wire fencing attached to a wood framework. A living screen provides some privacy and blocks sunlight. For more information on living screens, see the HP book, *Hedges, Screens and Espaliers.*

Gallery Of Fences, Walls And Gates

This section features examples of fences, gates and walls from various regions of the United States. Designs are presented that illustrate basic concepts. The emphasis is on one or two principles that are treated in an outstanding way.

The designs shown are the result of imaginative thinking. They were built to solve unique problems. The essential functions and spatial relationships with existing elements in the landscape were worked out first. Specific details and materials were determined next. Decorative details were usually integrated with the home's architecture. The designs often reflect the regional landscape and local traditions.

Some designs were created by landscape architects, others by homeowners. Use these examples as ideas and guidelines for your purposes.

TRIED AND TRUE

The ancient wall design in the photograph below is suited to large properties. The wall is placed along boundary lines. Livestock are prevented from wandering in or out of the area.

Old rock walls built of native stone contribute to and reflect the character of their area. The stones are usually cleared from fields in the area.

The method of wall construction, *coursed ashlar* or *random rubble,* is a local tradition. Coursed ashlar walls are built several *courses* or layers high using square-cut stones called *ashlar.*

Random-rubble walls are built using pieces of different-size rocks. If rock is too expensive in your part of the country, consider *veneer.* Veneer is thin pieces of native stone attached to a concrete-block wall. This creates an appearance that blends with the environment.

Low walls can be used to help create level terraces on sloping sites. Plants growing over walls can integrate the structure into the landscape. Low walls are used to retain plants around a patio. The walls make gardening and cleaning easy.

Large stones are placed along the base course in this random-rubble drywall. Wall has a steep *batter,* or pitch, to provide stability. Moss and lichen growth blend wall into the landscape and show age.

Old fence design of double posts and rails is strong and easy to build. This type of fence is suited for large landscapes and rural settings.

Board texture on low, concrete retaining wall is obtained by using rough-sawn lumber vertically in the formwork. Sand-blast boards to accentuate wood grain. Another way to achieve a similar effect is to use textured-plywood forms.

Low, wood-panel walls at left are easy to build. Add a wide wood cap for a garden seat and use walls to terrace a slope. Panel walls make excellent raised-bed retainers.

Traditional design of white picket fence is adaptable to many landscapes. Variations in basic design can make the fence simple and plain or ornate and detailed.

New Orleans "corn fence" is one of the most-famous wrought-iron fences in the world.

The traditional white picket fence in the photograph above is an excellent example of a basic fence design. Picket fences can be plain and inexpensive or ornate with costly details. Picket fences are favorite designs throughout New England and parts of the East and Midwest.

Wrought-iron fences are characteristic of both Spanish and Victorian architectural styles. These fences are usually identified with the classic New Orleans-style patio. Wrought iron is a type of iron that contains slag and a little carbon. It is tough, ductile and resistant to corrosion. The majority of wrought-iron fences available today are really cast-iron or welded metal.

Metal fencing—prefabricated, custom-made or antique—has an airy, open appearance. It permits light and air to enter. Metal fencing is especially practical for enclosing swimming-pool areas. Simple metal fencing in different colors was popular in Art Deco design in the 1930s.

Blue, ornamental metal fence on top of low, poured-concrete wall is simple but elegant.

Chain-link fences are popular for homeowners wanting security and privacy at an economical price. These fences are easy to install. Privacy can be achieved by covering chain-link fencing with vines or decorative strips. Chain-link fences keep children and pets in and intruders out. The fence in the photograph at right is practical and attractive.

The post-and-rail fence below is attractive and makes a useful boundary marker or decorative accent. Post-and-rail fences will not keep children or pets from wandering.

Unadorned chain-link fence is attractive. It provides boundary definition and security for children or pets.

Tall, three-rail fence can be used to contain livestock, serve as a boundary marker or as decoration in the landscape.

The attractive gate pictured at right is a small section of lattice. The gateway begins at the arch of vines. Low hedges add dimension to a flat path. The path leads back to the airy, open garden. The gate's location back from the major walkway ensures privacy. Plantings help to emphasize the entry. Placement of a fence back from the corner of a house downplays the gate's importance and reduces the gate's impact on the house.

A fresh white fence and arbor define the major entry and add a dramatic accent to the low, ranch-style house, page 23. The gateway improves the home's appearance and spotlights the front-door location.

The offset baffle-fence sections screen another entrance that leads to a family-room patio. This arrangement of baffles conceals the patio and makes the gate unnecessary except for security. The slat-gate design and matching fence insert improve air circulation. Both entries are lighted at night.

Vertical lattice is easy to cut to fit. Screening effect results from close spacing of lath. Low gate at right looks like part of fence.

View-blocking arrangement of baffle fence sections make a gate unnecessary except for security.

Left: Small screen creates two separate entryways and ensures privacy to both. Post anchors are inserted in mortar joints between paving bricks.

Below: Screen fence insert and matching gate encourage air circulation through a tiny patio. White brightens the area and a light marks the entry at night.

This courtyard is formed by walls of buildings. The size of the enclosed space is proportional to the height of walls.

Courtyards evolved from open interior spaces enclosed by building walls. A colonnade derived from Greek and Roman courtyards encloses this medieval-style courtyard at The Cloisters, a branch of the New York Metropolitan Museum of Art in New York City.

Two-part Dutch gate with a doorknob and doorbell may be opened in one or two sections. Open door allows view of the interior courtyard.

COURTYARDS

A private area in any garden creates a quiet retreat and makes garden space more usable. A courtyard or entry court created with fences or walls can achieve a balance between public exposure and private seclusion. This semipublic transition zone may be open with only a suggestion of enclosure. The courtyard area can be completely secure with gates and an intercom system or video cameras.

Courtyards are found in many cultures. Modern courtyards originated in ancient Greek and Roman atriums and the courtyards of monasteries and Moorish gardens of the Middle Ages. Courtyards came with the Spanish settlers to Mexico, California and the southwestern United States in the form of the patio. In Louisiana, the Spanish patio received a French accent to become the distinctive New Orleans-style patio.

Always check local building codes before constructing courtyards. Ordinances may restrict height of fences or walls or establish property line setback requirements.

Obtaining a variance from local zoning regulations may require submitting detailed plans and letters from neighbors stating approval of the plans. If it is impossible to get a variance, the height of low walls or fences may be extended by planting hedges to grow above them. Check local ordinances regarding hedges first. Screen plantings are a low-maintenance alternative to fences or walls.

In the photograph at left the courtyard behind the two-piece Dutch gate is a transition zone between public and private areas. The top half of the gate can be opened to extend a welcome to visitors, or it can be closed for complete privacy. Visitors must ring a doorbell by the gate for entry to the yard. This design basically extends the front door to the street.

Right: Plantings are clustered in a courtyard for ease of maintenance and to provide a visual focal point.

SHAPED BY WALLS

In the photographs at right and below, walls have shaped the garden, changing it from a roughly sloping site into usable outdoor spaces. These outdoor spaces are closely related to adjacent interior areas. Retaining walls hold soil and create two separate areas for different activities. The open, spacious quality of the garden encourages a link between the two areas.

Decorative brick columns define a stairway to the formal, raised-fountain area. The fountain area is located on the same level as a new sunroom addition. The steps are lighted by recessed fixtures placed in the brick walls. A simple brick cap makes an attractive shadow line.

Reinforcing in the concrete steps extends into the wall to tie steps and wall together. Concrete material provides contrast to the simulated used brick. Concrete edges the paving and forms the upper-level fountain.

A lower entertainment and barbecue area is on the same level as the family room. Brickwork is detailed by brown, *raked-mortar joints*. See the

illustrations on page 103 for details on mortar joints. The barbecue unit uses standard wall-construction techniques and is placed on a concrete footing. See page 94 for details on wall construction with bricks. The arbor posts are anchored in *concrete collars* below the paving. See pages 41 and 42 for construction details of concrete collars.

Above: Brick retaining walls create two garden levels linked by low steps. Columns emphasize the change of grade. Concealed lighting in wall makes the steps safe at night.

Below: Lower terrace includes space for outdoor cooking, dining and relaxing. Wood arbor provides support for growing vines.

Japanese sleeve gates are attached to metal runners normally used for sliding-glass doors.

Attractive gateway in a Japanese sleeve fence creates a good impression on visitors. Gates slide into fence. Rustic look of fence adds to appeal.

WELCOMING GATES

The impressive gates in the photograph above are set in a Japanese sleeve fence. The gates welcome people to this Hawaiian garden and tell visitors the residents are creative and friendly.

Each gate slides on runners through a guiding track. The track is set flush with the paving level. Rustic, large-scale posts, a little roof and boards with battens on edge give this fence a distinctive appearance.

Each element in the entry design has been carefully considered, including the plantings.

The white-and-blue sunburst gate in the photograph at right is attractive and functional. A jog or offset in the fence creates an entry stage. The offset lets the gate swing open without blocking the sidewalk. The low hedge behind the fence provides a wall of foliage to separate courtyard and city street.

Meticulous craftsmanship allows the gates to open and close smoothly.

Wooden channel tracks inserted in the paving guide the lap-joint gates.

Right: Entry stage shaped from a jog in the fence permits these fan-shape gates to swing clear of the sidewalk.

SERENE SMALL SPACE

In the photograph at right, efficient use of small spaces, green plants and naturally weathered wood create this garden's pleasing Oriental quality.

Parts of the garden have been extended into the driveway. Large areas of exposed-aggregate paving and two gates make the garden accessible to vehicles. One gate is for people and one is for automobiles. Both gates are detailed the same as the screen fencing. The design makes both gates practically disappear. This technique is useful in small spaces where numerous elements compete for attention and produce a sense of clutter. A storage area is concealed in the fence. The storage area is accessible from two sides.

The see-through quality of slat fencing provides a semipublic transition zone between public street and private garden. The transition between the outdoor garden and the indoor area is made by a low, narrow Japanese deck, called an *engawa*.

Weathered, gray wood in this fence recedes into the background. Slats allow breezes and light to enter garden.

Above: Slat-fence gate gives visitors a glimpse of interior garden, but provides privacy and security for the inhabitants. Gate blends in with fence.

Right: Driveway gate swings open to provide limited auto access. Trash enclosure is accessible from both sides and is practically invisible in the garden.

OUTDOOR ROOMS

Different gate and fence styles have been combined to create several outdoor rooms. The outdoor rooms in the photographs below extend the indoor-living areas of this remodeled one-room schoolhouse.

Although the lot is small and irregularly shaped, separate gardens seem to expand the area. Both areas offer different places for a variety of activities. The size and style of the outdoor rooms reflect the activities of adjacent indoor areas. Each outdoor room is two or three times larger than the corresponding indoor space.

The streetside entry invites visitors inside. Slat-fence siding is fastened to a grid of 2x4s. The grid alters the siding pattern. The slat design is repeated in the gate. Siding is painted to match the house trim. A roof and *finials* have been added for entry emphasis. Finials are the decorative tips of fence or post uprights. The gateway functions as the front door and opens on a citrus-filled entry court. The court is an extension of the inside foyer.

The courtyard fence of lattice, diagonal boards and open grillwork was designed to complement two special gates. The gates were recycled from the original front doors. A black, painted fence-cap ties the courtyard's two fence styles together.

Entry courtyard behind streetside gates is an extension of the inside foyer.

Fence was designed to complement antique gates. Gates are recycled from the original schoolhouse doors.

Gates lead from entry courtyard to a large, private garden. The garden is an extension of the living room.

PRIVACY IS NOT THE OBJECTIVE

A glass screen provides views and helps create a warm microclimate in a yard or patio. The screen blocks wind but permits sun to shine through. This combination of functions is good at a beach or lakefront. Although outsiders can see in as easily as residents can see out, a feeling of privacy is provided by the frames holding the glass panels. Framing enhances the feeling of protection obtained by blocking the wind. Raised platforms support the decks and patio, providing additional separation.

The glass screen in the two top photographs is attached to the top of a low brick retaining wall. The screen permits a spectacular view. The wall creates a level terrace and encloses a small paved patio. The wall blocks a view of the road between beach and house. Trimmed dwarf-ivy frames the view. Wooden frames are braced by metal brackets attached to the wall. A windbreak of Monterey cypress trees helps shelter the terrace.

The glass screen pictured at bottom right defines several spaces. One space is used for a cactus collection. The area shown is warm enough for growing potted citrus. The arbor on top of the glass screen breaks and deflects the turbulent flow of wind. The arbor also shelters the decks. Glass doors open on a path leading to the beach.

Plastic sheets and glass blocks are alternatives to glass screens. These translucent materials allow light to enter, but offer greater privacy than clear glass.

Top, right: Clipped dwarf-ivy vine softens wood frames of glass screen. The screen shelters a brick terrace from breezes.

Center, right: Low brick retaining wall supports the glass screen. The screen is braced with metal brackets. Metal gates lead to the terrace and are fastened to simple brick columns.

Bottom, right: Glass panels framed with mitered trim pieces are attached to extended posts. Posts support an arbor that breaks turbulent wind force on exposed deck.

THE PERFECT SCREEN

The photograph at right shows how versatile screens can be. A deck was built to obtain usable outdoor space on a steeply sloping lot.

Enclosing the deck with a screen made the space semiprivate and enjoyable for the owners. The screen is designed and constructed with translucent plastic panels. The panels allow sunlight to penetrate, but block most of the wind.

Framing around a window in the screen accentuates and improves the view of the San Francisco-Oakland Bay bridge by blocking the rooftops in the foreground.

Right: Open window in a plastic-and-wood screen frames a view. Translucent plastic panels permit light to penetrate but block wind. Plastic panels are cheap and easy to install. They offer more privacy than glass.

Below: Interior view of courtyard shows bright, white stucco walls accentuated by colorful plants. Niche in wall can hold sculpture.

TIMELESS DESIGN

Stucco walls and gate in this courtyard were only a year old when the photograph above was taken. The walls are in harmony with the early California house and appear to be part of the original construction.

The garden was in front and the corner lot received plenty of sun but provided little privacy. The owners were reluctant to block views from the street with a high wall because the house is a local landmark.

A courtyard was the logical solution because it would provide privacy and be suited to the home's Spanish style.

Low courtyard walls allow much of the house to be seen. The detailed gate provides a visible replacement for that part of the house concealed behind the walls.

At the courtyard entry, the wall changes into a rustic pediment. The pediment duplicates the angle of the house roofline. The gateway arch and rough board gate are typical Spanish details.

Several coats of thickly troweled *stucco,* a mixture of sand and cement, were applied over a wood stud wall. The rough, textured stucco produced an adobelike appearance, characteris-

Tile-capped stucco wall enclosing courtyard forms a rustic pediment over the arched entry gate.

tic of old California. *Adobe* is a mixture of different clay soils and straw. It is used to make bricks, common in the Southwest.

A tile cap protects the wall top and matches the tile roof. Boards on each side of the gate arch support the thumb latch and hinges. The large iron strap hinges are ornamental.

SHADY GARDEN

Attractive details and natural wood combine to make the graceful lattice fence shown at right. The open fence keeps children and pets from wandering and still defines boundaries in a warm and friendly manner. Views are reduced without being obscured.

Open latticework allows light to penetrate into the shady yard. Breezes pass through the openings, a welcome feature in warm summer areas. The fence steps down a gentle slope, but the same type of fence can be used on flat sites.

Shrubs behind the fence increase privacy. An open-and-closed effect is created by vines. The narrow planting strip in front is used for low-maintenance perennial and bulb plantings. Elegant finials cap the posts.

SCREENED RETREAT

Shade is welcome in the warm climate of Atlanta, Georgia. Lattice panels and low retaining walls combine to produce this variation of a screened porch in the photograph below right. A shady retreat has been created beside the front door. Windows gain privacy and sun protection.

The lattice panels are framed by an open-lath pattern. The panels sit on top of a vine-covered retaining wall. The wall raises the entry paving to the same level as the door for an easy, indoor-outdoor flow of space.

Overhead beams support tall lattice panels and attach them to the house. The same shade of gray on the screens and front door harmonizes with the gray in house and wall brick. Matching lath shades placed over upper dormer windows screen sunlight.

This project was carefully designed to be small in scale. If the same screening style had been used around the entire garden, the impact of the design would have been reduced. Costs would have been much higher if more screen had been used.

Tall fencing located close to a house is usually within property line setback requirements. A building permit may be required in some areas.

This shady garden is enclosed by open lattice. Lattice admits warm sunlight or cooling breezes.

Beams tie screen panels to house. Finials top fenceposts.

Lattice panels screen front windows on this entry and create a gracious transition area between indoors and out.

Fence was painted to match house and trim. Creamy white highlights posts and lattice panels.

Inexpensive bamboo poles make a screen support under a stairway.

2

HOW TO BUILD FENCES

Attractive, white, painted fence reflects traditional style of surrounding community. Integrated plantings provide privacy screen and accent delicate pattern of fence.

Fences are available in many different sizes, shapes, designs and materials. Most fences are constructed on the same basic framework of *posts, rails* or *stringers,* and *siding* or *wire.* Posts are the vertical uprights. They support the horizontal rails, or *stringers.* Siding is the exterior material attached to the rails. Variations in materials and size can create different styles and designs. The basic elements remain the same.

Complete step-by-step directions for building a basic wooden fence are included in this chapter.

Fence-Building Basics

Step 1—Plot the location of the fence. Determine the proper spacing of posts, usually 8 feet apart or less. See page 36.

Step 2—Use preservatives to protect wood posts from decay. See page 38.

Step 3—Stake out post locations in the landscape. See page 38.

Step 4—Dig the postholes. See page 38.

Step 5—Cut, set and secure posts in the holes. See page 40.

Step 6—Cut rails or stringers and attach to posts. See page 43.

Step 7—Cut and attach siding or wire. See page 47.

Step 8—Optional: apply paint or finish. See page 49.

Left: Careful building techniques are important for an attractive, finished appearance. Setting posts vertically is important. Gate posts should be set deeper than regular fenceposts.

ANATOMY OF A FENCE

CAP, OPTIONAL

TOP RAIL

4x4 WOOD POST

SIDING BOARDS

BOTTOM RAIL

DADO JOINT

2" CLEARANCE

BUTT JOINT

GRAVEL OR CONCRETE COLLAR

GRAVEL BASE

Basic fence framework consists of posts, top and bottom rails, and wood or wire siding. Additional elements can include a middle supporting rail and top cap.

STEP 1:
PLOTTING THE FENCE

The proper placement of a fence on your property is important. Placement must meet all legal requirements for locations on or near property lines. It may be necessary to have property lines surveyed to determine their exact location.

It's important to plan the fence location to avoid obvious obstacles, such as trees or large rocks. You will need to locate underground utility lines, including sewer, water, electricity, gas and telephone. Don't start digging holes until you are certain there are no utilities in the immediate area.

After you've decided where the fence will be located, measure the fence's approximate length. Don't forget to allow space in the overall length for one or more gates.

Divide this length into equal intervals to determine proper post spacing. Intervals of 6 or 8 feet are the most common. Placing posts more than 8 feet apart is not recommended because rails can sag. Intervals of 6 or 8 feet allow you to use common sizes of precut lumber in even lengths. Precut lumber is lumber that comes from the

Rustic post-and-rail fence attractively defines edge of planting and drive. Short rail segments follow contours and accentuate slope. Bottom rail of this two-rail, mortise-and-tenon fence is concealed by ivy.

lumberyard in specific lengths, usually 6 feet, 8 feet, 10 feet or 12 feet.

Fenceposts are available in several different sizes and any length. Most fences use a 4x4 post, but larger posts, 6x6 or 8x8, can be used. Rails are usually 2x4s in 6-, 8- or 10-foot lengths.

If the fence length is not an exact multiple of the interval, you have several alternatives. You can divide the length into equal spaces slightly longer or shorter than the interval. Shortening or lengthening the interval can result in some waste if you use precut lumber. To avoid waste, try to establish intervals in common precut lumber lengths.

If one section of the fence is shorter, use it for the gate location or make that section of the fence smaller. This odd-sized fence section is the most economical design if you are using standard lumber lengths.

If you are cutting posts, rails and siding as you build the fence, you have more flexibility in determining the interval size. Cutting lumber yourself allows you to make small adjustments in the overall length or height of the fence.

Measuring for fencepost location requires measuring tape. Use stakes to mark location of postholes.

PLOTTING A FENCE

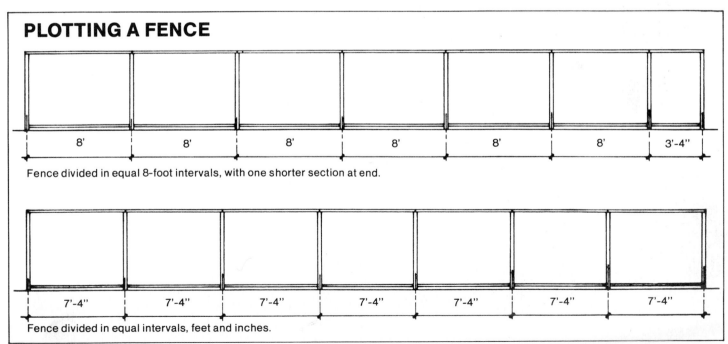

| 8' | 8' | 8' | 8' | 8' | 8' | 3'-4" |

Fence divided in equal 8-foot intervals, with one shorter section at end.

| 7'-4" | 7'-4" | 7'-4" | 7'-4" | 7'-4" | 7'-4" | 7'-4" |

Fence divided in equal intervals, feet and inches.

Determining location for fenceposts requires knowing entire length of fence, plus space for gates. The first method, top, requires dividing the fence length in regular intervals of 6 or 8 feet between posts. Any remaining interval less than 6 or 8 feet is either used for a gate or a shorter fence section. This method makes best use of standard lengths of precut fencing lumber. The second method, bottom, requires dividing the fence length into equal intervals. This method requires a considerable amount of measuring, cutting and fitting pieces together. It also wastes a lot of lumber.

Here is one way to treat fenceposts with preservative. Fill a deep container with posts and add chemical preservative to the level of the below-ground portion plus 2 inches. Periodically check level of chemical as you repeat operation. Using pressure-treated wood eliminates this step.

STEP 2:
PRESERVING POSTS

All wooden posts must be chemically treated to prevent decay. Redwood and other naturally decay-resistant woods *do* deteriorate with time. Buy pressure-treated posts, or chemically treat posts yourself. Treat posts by soaking the below-ground part of the post, plus an extra 2 inches, in a wood preservative. Cut-ends of pressure-treated posts should be soaked in preservative. Paint metal posts with a rust-resistant primer paint. See page 158 for more information on preservatives for wood.

STEP 3:
LOCATE POSTS

Mark both end points of the fence with wooden stakes. Tie string tightly between stakes. Next, measure and locate positions for all posts between the end posts and mark these locations with stakes. Measure the intervals between them with a tape or lay precut rails in line along the ground between the end stakes. The structural strength and finished appearance of the fence depends on accurate positioning of posts.

STEP 4:
DIG POSTHOLES

All wooden fenceposts should be set with approximately 1/3 of the total length buried in the ground. This ratio is especially important on corner-posts, posts that support heavy weights or posts that must withstand strong wind. Using this rule, a 6-foot-high fence requires a 9-foot-long post.

Another common guideline is to sink posts 2 feet deep for 5-foot-high fences, 2-1/2 feet deep for 6-foot-high fences and 3-1/2 feet deep for 8-foot-high fences. Use precut fenceposts, or cut to length as required. Gateposts and endposts should be set deeper in the ground for additional stability.

Dig postholes 6 inches deeper than the depth actually needed. Fill this extra depth with 5 or 6 inches of gravel or a large stone to aid drainage. Gravel prevents concrete from sealing off post bottoms. Posts can be anchored better if you make the hole slightly larger at the bottom than the top.

Dig the holes vertically straight and in the correct locations. Use a hand or power auger if the soil is free of stones. Use a clamshell-type digger if the soil is rocky. Hardware stores or home centers rent these tools. It's difficult to dig a deep, narrow hole with a shovel.

The size or diameter of the posthole depends on the size of the post, the type of *footing* used and the type of soil. Footings are the materials, usually concrete, placed under and around posts or walls to support them. Posts are usually 4x4'' or 6x6''. See pages 40 and 41 for detailed information on footings.

For gravel-filled footings in sandy or average soils, dig postholes slightly larger than the posts. In clay soils, dig postholes twice the diameter of posts. Posts anchored with a *concrete collar* need a hole two or three times the diameter of the post. A concrete collar is a layer of concrete placed in the posthole around the post. The concrete extends slightly above ground to help shed water. See page 41. A 4x4 post needs a collar at least 9 inches wide. This means the posthole should be dug 9 inches wide or wider. The sides of the hole form the concrete collar mold.

Left to right: Tools for digging postholes. Hand-operated clamshell digger is for rocky soil. Power auger digs holes in hard soil. It requires two people to operate it. Hand-operated auger twists through rock-free soil, boring and scooping out earth.

SOIL TYPES

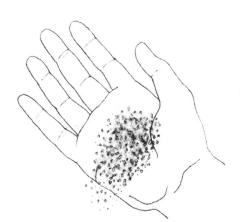

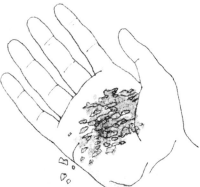

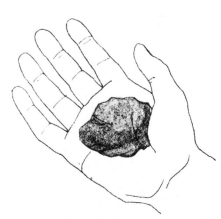

Sandy Soil
Loose and single-grained with individual grains readily visible. Moistened clump should fall apart.

Loam Soil
Moistened clump of soil will stick together, then break apart into irregular clumps. Soil has gritty feel from sand content.

Clay Soil
Feels greasy or sticky when wet. Wet clay soil sticks to a shovel and can be squeezed through fingers to form a ribbon.

Post alignment is a critical step. Set the endpost or cornerpost vertical in alignment with the other endpost or cornerpost. Attach two strings between posts at top and bottom and stretch strings tight. Have a helper plumb each post using strings as guides. Fill holes with concrete or backfill.

GRAVEL AND EARTH FOOTING

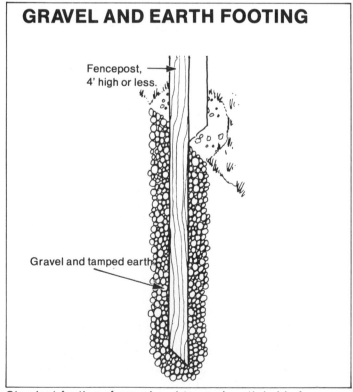

Fencepost, 4' high or less.

Gravel and tamped earth.

Simplest footing of gravel and tamped earth holds fencepost in position. This method is not recommended for fences more than 4 feet high.

CLEATS AND GRAVEL FOOTING

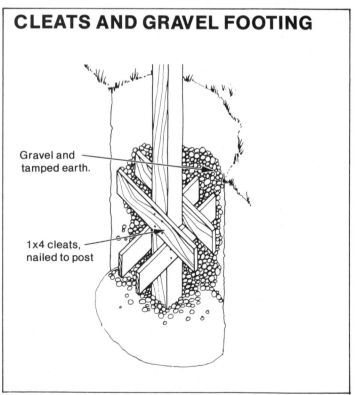

Gravel and tamped earth.

1x4 cleats, nailed to post

To add stability to posts in light or sandy soils, make cleats of preservative-treated wood. Attach cleats to posts with aluminum nails. Fill hole with gravel and tamped earth.

STEP 5:
SET AND SECURE POSTS

Set one cornerpost first. Use a *carpenter's level* or a *plumb bob* to align the post 90° vertically. A carpenter's level is a length of wood or metal with vials of liquid sealed in glass or plastic. When the air bubble inside the vial is centered, the object being checked is horizontally or vertically positioned. A plumb bob is a lead weight hung at the end of a line. Use it to determine whether a post or wall is vertical.

Have a helper hold the post and shovel in 2 or 3 inches of gravel. Tamp gravel down with a 2x4. This gravel is for drainage, not bracing.

Brace post in a vertical position with temporary braces made from wood scraps. Braces should be attached to two or three sides of the fencepost and attached to stakes driven in the ground. See illustration on page 42.

Setting fenceposts requires care in vertical alignment. A concrete collar is the most effective way to anchor posts. Temporary bracing is tacked to two faces of the post to hold it securely while wet concrete sets and cures. Readjust bracing to keep post vertically plumb. Allow concrete to cure 2 days.

CONCRETE-COLLAR FOOTING

FENCEPOST

Slope top of footing to shed water.

Gravel base, approximately 6" deep.

Post extends through concrete collar into gravel.

Minimum width of collar is equal to twice width of post.

Solid concrete collars are the best post footings. Never seal the bottom of a post in concrete. Be sure post bottom rests in gravel or on a large rock. Slope concrete collar away from post for drainage. A collar placed slightly below soil level is more attractive but less water-resistant. Check to be sure post is vertically plumb before concrete sets. Brace posts with temporary braces if desired. Allow concrete to cure for at least two days before attaching fence rails.

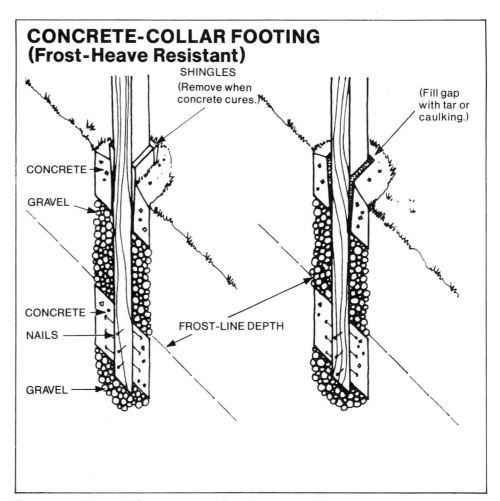

CONCRETE-COLLAR FOOTING (Frost-Heave Resistant)

SHINGLES (Remove when concrete cures.)

(Fill gap with tar or caulking.)

CONCRETE

GRAVEL

CONCRETE

NAILS

FROST-LINE DEPTH

GRAVEL

This method is used for concrete collars in areas with deep frost-line depths. Dig posthole 1 foot deeper than frost-line depth. Place small amount of gravel in hole and set post. Add concrete to frost-line depth. Fill posthole to 6 inches below top with gravel. Add concrete until it is just above top of posthole. Optional expansion collar can be made from shingle scraps coated with oil and placed around four sides of post. Fill remainder of hole with concrete and remove shingles after concrete has cured. Fill opening with tar.

After bracing and adding gravel to the hole, recheck vertical alignment with the level or plumb bob. Fill the hole with gravel, soil or concrete. Postholes can be filled with earth or a combination of earth and gravel. The fence should be less than 4 feet tall and posts set in average, stable soils.

If soil fill is used, short pieces of 1x2 wood cleats should be nailed at several locations on the lower 1/3 of the post. Wood cleats provide added stability in light or sandy soils. Place backfill, a combination of earth and gravel, around cleats and tamp backfill in place. See page 40.

Set taller posts in concrete collars to provide additional stability for heavy fences. See page 41.

When the first cornerpost has been set and aligned, set the other cornerpost firmly, but not permanently in the hole. Stretch a string between the two posts. Then set posts between the cornerposts in position. Carefully align and brace middle posts vertically. Make sure posts are spaced at proper intervals. The tops of all posts should be the same height.

After all posts are set and aligned, add gravel or soil to each posthole. Tamp the fill down every few inches.

If you use concrete collars, leave the top 5 or 6 inches of the hole empty. Then fill the hole with concrete until it is slightly above ground. Slope the top of the concrete collar away from the post. The slope lets water drain away from the post, slowing down decay at the post's base. Leave temporary braces in place until the concrete collar has cured and fence rails have been added.

Concrete collars should be used for metal posts or gateposts, especially where strong wind threatens stability or if soils are unstable. Clay soils and regions of abnormal frost heaving are examples of unstable soils. If a fence will be taller than 4 feet high, concrete collars provide extra stability.

STEP 6:
ATTACH RAILS, STRINGERS OR WIRE

After posts are in place and the concrete has cured, the next step is to attach the top rail, or stringer. This rail is usually placed flat on top of posts to keep the fence in alignment.

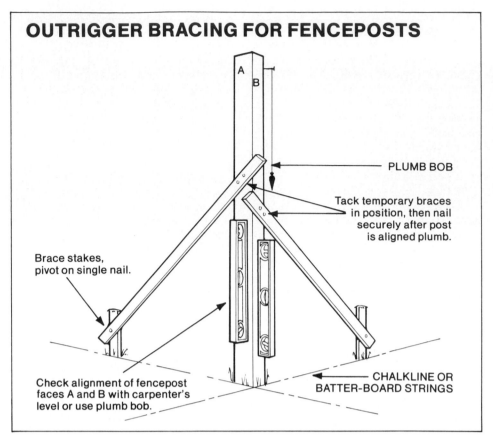

OUTRIGGER BRACING FOR FENCEPOSTS

A
B

PLUMB BOB

Tack temporary braces in position, then nail securely after post is aligned plumb.

Brace stakes, pivot on single nail.

Check alignment of fencepost faces A and B with carpenter's level or use plumb bob.

CHALKLINE OR BATTER-BOARD STRINGS

This method is commonly called the one-person method for bracing posts. Position two stakes in firm soil near posthole. Nail a wood brace to each stake. Place post in hole, resting base on gravel or rock at bottom. Align post with batter-board strings or chalklines as shown. Use level or plumb bob to make face A of post vertically plumb. Tack brace lightly to post. Then plumb face B of the post. Tack remaining brace lightly to post. Recheck plumb of both face A and B for vertical. Retack braces as necessary. Nail braces securely to post. Anchor post with concrete collar, gravel or earth.

Mixing Concrete For Collars

Mixing concrete to make collars for fenceposts is easy. All you need is a large bucket, tub or wheelbarrow, shovel and trowel.

The four basic ingredients to make concrete are: cement, sand, gravel and water. If you don't want to purchase concrete ingredients separately, premix concrete is available at building supply outlets.

Premix concrete has the basic ingredients of cement, sand and gravel packaged together in a 90-pound sack. To make concrete, add water and mix together.

The recommended formula for mixing concrete collars is one part cement, three parts sand and five parts gravel. Mix all dry ingredients together. Add water a little at a time until the concrete is stiff and packs into a ball in your hand. If the concrete is too stiff, add a little more water. If it is too liquid, add more dry sand and cement. Each posthole requires approximately 2/3 cubic foot of concrete. Each cubic foot of dry ingredients is equal to 2/3 cubic foot of wet concrete.

The fencepost should already be positioned and braced in the hole before mixing the concrete. Place the post in the hole as described on page 41. Pour the concrete in the posthole on top of the gravel.

Tamp the concrete to displace any air bubbles. Tamping helps to redistribute sand and gravel aggregate. Extend the concrete slightly above soil level. Use a mason's trowel to slope concrete away from the post for water drainage.

Check alignment of the post before the concrete sets and reposition the post to 90° vertical if necessary. Leave posts undisturbed for 48 hours to allow concrete to cure.

Use precut lumber for rails if possible, or cut rails to the length required.

A *lap joint, dado joint* or *mortise-and-tenon joint* may be used where rails meet at the posts. You can also use a *butt joint* by placing ends of rails together. Some wood joints provide strength. Other joints give a finished appearance.

Make all joint cuts after posts are set. Use a portable electric sabre saw or reciprocating saw to make cuts. See pages 44-46 for common woodworking joints.

Fasteners—Nails are most commonly used to attach rails, stringers and siding to wooden fences. Where extra strength is needed, metal connectors are used to reinforce joints. Connectors can be attached with nails or round-head wood screws. All fasteners should be galvanized or otherwise rust-resistant. Fasteners used in fence and wall construction are shown on pages 82 and 156.

When the top rail is in place, measure down the post to position the bottom rail. The bottom rail should be 6 to 12 inches above ground. Use one of the woodworking joints shown on page 44 or 45. Setting the bottom rail on edge gives twice the strength of a rail laid flat. It also helps prevent sagging.

Dado and mortise-and-tenon joints can be cut before setting posts. See illustration on page 46. Be precise. Precutting joints leaves little room for error in setting posts.

Toenailing rails and using butt joints is adequate for a light fence. Toenailing means driving nails at an angle through the side and end of one board into the surface of another board. Wooden blocks placed under a toenailed butt joint will increase the joint's supportive strength.

For a stronger fence, add a middle rail between the top and bottom rail. See page 52 for details on modifying a basic fence framework.

Before attaching rails to posts, apply paint or wood preservative to cut-ends of posts and rails where they will touch.

Wooden 4x4 posts are treated with preservative and anchored in concrete collars. Posts do not extend above pickets in this design. Top rail spans post tops. Bottom rail uses a butt joint and is toenailed. Rails were added after concrete had cured several days.

Common Woodworking Joints

There are several basic woodworking joints that can be used for attaching rails to wooden posts. The joint used will depend on the type of fence being built.

Butt Joint—This joint is relatively easy to make. The end of one board is placed against the end or side of another board or post. It may require some support blocks underneath to give additional strength. Butt joints can be made with rails placed horizontally or vertically.

Lap Joint—This is one of the easiest joints to make. It requires nailing the rail to the side or top of the post and butting the ends of rails together. The lap joint can be a top lap or side lap joint. A variation on the top lap features mitered rail ends for corners.

Dado Joint—A dado joint is similar to the lap joint, except the rails are grooved or set into the post, instead of being nailed to the surface. Rails may be placed on edge or flat.

Mortise-And-Tenon Joint—This is a tight-fitting wood joint. It is neater in appearance than a butt or a dado joint. It requires skill and effort to make the *mortise* in the post. A mortise is a hole that goes all or part-way through a piece of wood. A mortise partway through the post is called a *closed mortise*. The *tenon* is the projecting part cut on the end of a piece of wood. The tenon is inserted into the mortise hole. A *through mortise-and-tenon joint* is similar to the closed mortise-and-tenon joint, except the hole goes all the way through the post. Rails slide in the slot and rest on top of each other. This joint is common in split-rail fence construction. See page 46.

COMMON WOOD JOINTS

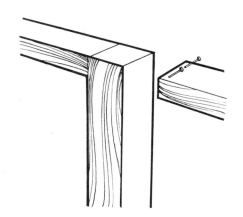

Butt Joint (horizontal rail)
Common butt joint uses rails butted flat against post and nailed in position. This joint is weak.

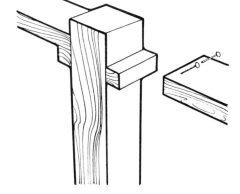

Block Butt Joint
Block joint uses a small block of wood placed under the basic butt joint to support rail. This joint provides greater strength for toe-nailed rails.

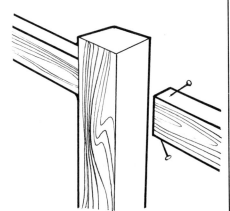

Butt Joint (vertical rail)
A simple variation of the butt joint. Rails are placed vertically against post and nails are driven through rail into post.

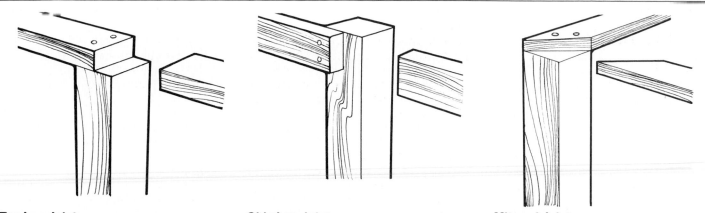

Top Lap Joint
Strong and water-resistant joint. Top rail ends are butted together and centered on top of posts. Rails are placed horizontally flat; may tend to sag.

Side Lap Joint
Top or bottom rail ends are butted together and centered across side of post. Side lap joint is not as strong as top lap joint. Vertical rails minimize sagging.

Mitered Joint
This is a variation on the top lap joint. Use at cornerposts for top rails and caps. It gives a finished look to top rails at corners. Rails may sag.

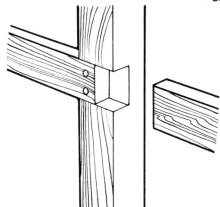

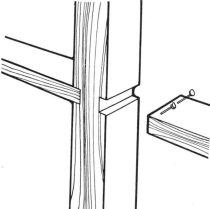

Dado Joint (rail on edge)
Dado joints are strong and easy to make. Dadoes, or grooves, are cut in the side of posts to accept rails. Rails are placed on edge. Rails are butted together, centered in dado and nailed. Vertical rails minimize sagging.

Dado Joint (rails laid flat)
This dado joint is also strong and easy to make. Cut dadoes in posts to accept the end of rails laid flat. Insert rails and toenail in place. Rails laid flat may tend to sag.

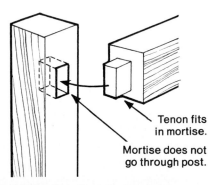

Tenon fits in mortise.

Mortise does not go through post.

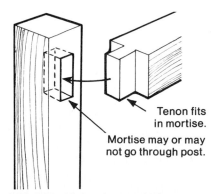

Tenon fits in mortise.

Mortise may or may not go through post.

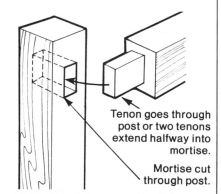

Tenon goes through post or two tenons extend halfway into mortise.

Mortise cut through post.

Closed Mortise-And-Tenon Joint
This mortise-and-tenon joint requires that the top edges of the tenon be cut to produce shoulders on the rail. This joint has the tenon extended partway through the mortise in the post.

Basic Mortise-And-Tenon Joint
The mortise-and-tenon joint is one of the strongest joints used in fence construction. The tenon is cut on the rail end and should be 1/3 the thickness of the rail. It may or may not extend completely through the post mortise. The mortise is cut in the post to accept the tenon. The mortise should be as deep as the tenon is long.

Through Mortise-And-Tenon Joint
Made in the same manner as the closed mortise and tenon, except the tenon extends completely through the mortise. In fence construction, the mortise may extend completely through the post, but tenons for joining rails extend halfway through the mortise and butt together.

Post-And-Rail Fence Construction

Post-and-rail fences are usually constructed with mortised posts and tenoned rails. These posts and rails are available precut, but you can make your own as shown in the illustration below. Three basic variations are possible.

The method shown in the center illustration requires a through mortise cut the size of one rail tenon in the post. Half tenons are cut on the end of each rail and rail ends overlap each other in the mortise.

The method shown in the right illustration requires a through mortise cut the depth of both rails in the post. Rails are then placed one on top of the other in the mortise.

The method shown in the bottom illustration requires a mortise cut the width of two rails in the post. Rails are placed side by side in the mortise.

Split rails and rough, squared posts are available with precut mortises. Tenon length is usually equal to post width.

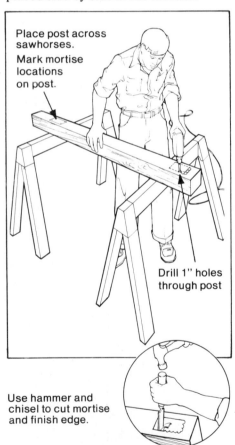

Place post across sawhorses.

Mark mortise locations on post.

Drill 1" holes through post

Use hammer and chisel to cut mortise and finish edge.

MORTISING A POST

You can cut mortises in fenceposts. Mark the location of mortises on posts. Make mortises the same size as the tenons or rails. Drill holes through the post to rough out mortise. Use a hammer and sharp chisel to finish cutting the mortise and smooth edges.

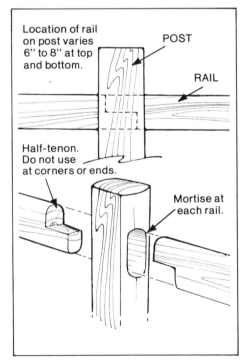

Location of rail on post varies 6" to 8" at top and bottom.

POST

RAIL

Half-tenon. Do not use at corners or ends.

Mortise at each rail.

This mortise-and-tenon joint requires cutting a half tenon on the end of each rail. Rails overlap inside the mortise.

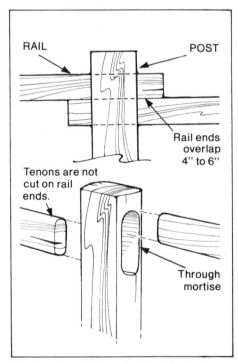

RAIL

POST

Rail ends overlap 4" to 6"

Tenons are not cut on rail ends.

Through mortise

Mortise is cut the depth of both fence rails. Rails are placed one on top of another inside the mortise.

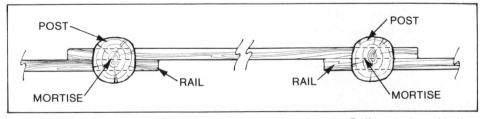

POST

POST

RAIL

RAIL

MORTISE

MORTISE

In this fence style, the mortise is cut the width of both rails. Rails are placed in the mortised post side by side.

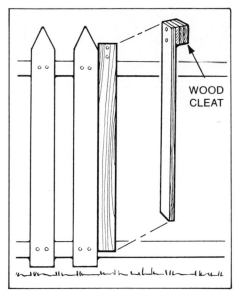

WOOD CLEAT

Here is a simple method for uniform spacing of pickets for fences. Use an extra picket or wooden cleat and attach a block of wood to the top as shown. Align the first picket vertically plumb and attach it to the fence rails. Place the spacer guide against the first picket, hanging it on the rail. Then place the second picket against the guide and attach the picket to rails. Repeat until all pickets are in place.

STEP 7: ATTACHING SIDING OR WIRE

Wooden siding is usually installed in a vertical rather than horizontal pattern. The vertical pattern makes better use of post spacing. Horizontal siding emphasizes sloping ground. Pickets, grapestakes or vertical boards should reach from below the bottom rail to the top rail. Keep the bottom of siding at least 2 inches above ground. You can extend siding above the top rail for additional height.

Wood shrinks with exposure to the elements. Boards placed tight against each other will eventually separate. For a completely solid fence with no gaps, use *tongue-and-groove* plywood siding or boards. Tongue-and-groove plywood has a projecting *tongue* on one edge of the 4x8' sheet and a *groove* on the other edge. The tongue on one sheet of plywood fits in the groove on another adjoining sheet of plywood.

To maintain uniform spaces between vertical boards, cut a slat of wood the width of the desired opening. Attach a small wooden cleat to the top of this spacer slat. Nail the first fence board to the rails and then hang the spacer next to it on the rail. Place the second board against the spacer and nail it to the rails. Repeat this spacing process until all vertical boards are in place. See the illustration at left.

Welded-wire or chain-link fencing is attached to top and bottom rails by different methods. If welded wire is used, it is attached to rails with U-shaped wire staples. Chain-link fencing is usually tied to metal rails with wire. See page 51 for details.

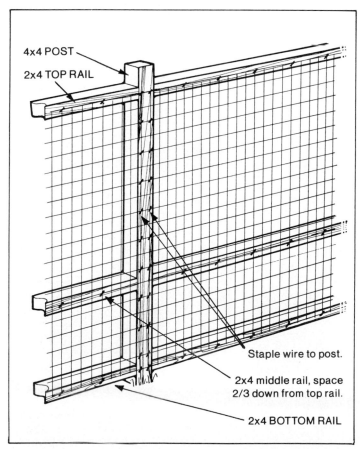

4x4 POST

2x4 TOP RAIL

Staple wire to post.

2x4 middle rail, space 2/3 down from top rail.

2x4 BOTTOM RAIL

Welded-wire fencing is attached to wooden framework with wire staples. Stretch wire over framework as described at right and align wire in postion. Attach wire with fence staples.

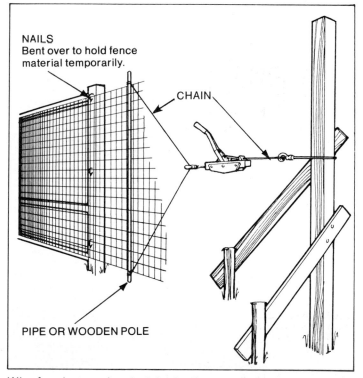

NAILS
Bent over to hold fence material temporarily.

CHAIN

PIPE OR WOODEN POLE

Wire fencing can be stretched using several methods. Place a braced dummy post or heavy object, such as a car, at the end of the fence. Place a strong wooden pole or metal pipe vertically through the fence. Attach a chain to each end of the pipe. Use a commercial fence puller, available from rental centers, and attach it to the chain on the pipe. Attach another chain to the dummy post and fence puller. Adjust the fence puller until fence is tight. Attach fence to the framework.

Traditional design of waist-high, redwood picket fence requires precision construction to achieve neat look. Molded trim pieces cover the nails and spacers that hold pickets to rails. Pickets wrap around cornerpost.

Cut pickets and spacer blocks while concrete cures. Position a picket at each corner. Run a tight string between corner pickets as an alignment guide for all other picket tops. Nail pickets and spacers in position.

Check for plumb as you work. Uniformity and careful spacing is an important element in this design. After all pickets and spacers are nailed in position, cover spacer blocks with molded trim pieces. Use galvanized finishing nails.

Bucket is filled with square spacer blocks precut from the same 2x2 lumber as pickets. Spacers are nailed between each picket to top and bottom rail. Wheelbarrow holds precut pickets.

STEP 8:
APPLYING FINISHES

There are many finishes that will protect a fence. Finishes include bleach, clear sealers, stain and paint.

Leaving a fence to weather naturally is appropriate for decay-resistant woods. Redwood, cypress and cedar change to attractive gray shades as they are exposed to the weather.

Bleach gives redwood a quick, uniform weathered appearance. New redwood can be darkened by applying a solution of 1 part baking soda to 10 parts water. Apply weathering solutions with a brush.

Lumber that is not naturally resistant to decay tends to splinter with exposure to weather. Use a transparent sealer for these wood species.

Clear Sealers or water-resistant coatings are sometimes called *repellents*. They help prevent rain and moisture from soaking into woods. Apply repellents annually to preserve natural wood color for many years.

Film-forming finishes are not recommended. Shellac discolors and cracks when exposed to weather. Varnish may yellow and needs constant renewing. Urethane plastic varnishes are more durable, but they must be completely removed before applying a new coat.

Stain allows some qualities of wood to show through and still protects fences against weathering. Semi-transparent penetrating stains present a uniform appearance, allowing wood grain to show. Heavy-bodied stains cover wood grain but not texture.

Paint is an excellent wood preservative. Paint seals and protects wood surfaces. Use a durable, exterior wood-finish paint. Paint is available in both oil-base and water-emulsion types. Paint is not recommended for use on green or unseasoned lumber.

Natural redwood fence will age to a beautiful shade of gray as it weathers.

Stained cedar fence is protected from elements. Wood texture shows through stain.

Natural color of cedar fence is preserved by water-resistant sealer.

Painted wood fence has defects concealed by paint. Surface is protected from moisture.

Step 1: First step in chain-link fence installation is to plot location of fenceline and locate postholes.

Step 2: After post location has been determined, dig postholes with hand or power auger.

Step 3: Set metal posts in holes and pour concrete around posts.

Step 4: Align posts in concrete vertically plumb. Brace to maintain vertical alignment while concrete cures.

Chain-Link Fence Installation

A simple chain-link fence offers several advantages to the homeowner. It offers low maintenance, is long lasting and is inexpensive and easy to install. Most chain-link fences come in a kit that includes all materials needed, except for concrete.

Materials needed include the posts and rails, fence fabric, all essential hardware items, wire or wire clips, a gate and gate hardware, wood stakes and concrete.

Tools needed include a posthole digger, shovel, measuring tape, hammer, pliers and wire cutters, fence puller and assorted wrenches for nuts and bolts.

Follow the instructions outlined in the photographs on these two pages to install your chain-link fence.

Step 5: After concrete has cured for several days, attach metal top rails and hardware to the posts.

Step 6: Chain-link fencing can be stretched along fenceline after rails are attached to posts. Fence pullers can be rented, or use a block and tackle attached to your car.

Step 7: Chain-link fencing is attached to metal rails and posts with short pieces of wire or special clips. Keep fence material aligned with top rails.

Step 8: Attachment of gate is final step in installation procedure. Bolt support hardware to gatepost and then hang gate on hinge pins. Adjust gate latch as necessary.

Modifying Basic Fence Framework

The basic wood-fence framework of posts, rails and siding can be modified in many ways. Larger posts and rails may be substituted for 4x4s and 2x4s. Larger lumber makes the fence sturdier and creates a heavy appearance.

A middle rail may be added between the top and bottom rails to increase fence strength or to add a visual line. This line looks more pleasing if the rail is located approximately 2/3 of the way down between top and bottom rails.

A horizontal *cap* can be added to the top of the fence. A cap is a long piece of lumber that covers the top of a fence or wall. It can be the same or wider than the wall width. This cap protects post and board tops from water.

Siding can be placed on the rails vertically, horizontally or diagonally.

Boards may alternate from side to side or weave between posts. Siding boards can be different widths or thicknesses. See the examples below.

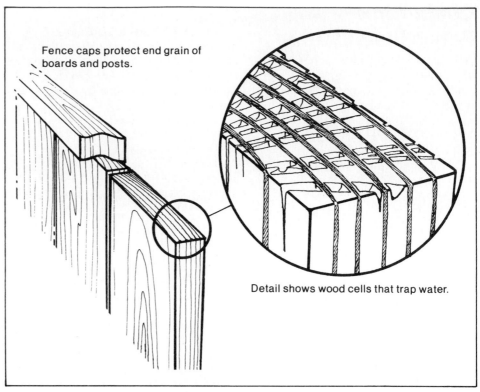

Fence caps protect end grain of boards and posts.

Detail shows wood cells that trap water.

Caps are often placed on the top edge of wood fences to protect the end grain of boards and posts from absorbing water.

Basic fence design has been modified by addition of vertical and horizontal siding to form a lattice-weave effect. Top fence cap adds decorative and practical touch.

Basket-weave fence is another modification of basic fence. Long, flexible, horizontal boards create a well-defined shadow effect.

Board-and-batten fence uses vertical board siding with edges butted together. Thin board battens cover butt joints and add texture and depth to design.

Simple two-rail fence is modified by addition of third middle rail. This fence provides boundary definition and live-stock restraint.

Horizontal-board fence forms solid wall-like structure. It blocks wind and provides shade and privacy. Design and painted surface match house.

Board-and-board fence is made from stained cedar. Design allows air circulation and still provides privacy. This fence looks the same on both sides and is called a *good-neighbor fence.*

Lumber

Lumber is one of the oldest building materials known. It is easy to work with, readily available throughout the world and versatile. These properties make lumber the most universally used building material.

Lumber is available in hardwoods or softwoods, depending on the species of tree from which it was milled.

Fences are usually constructed from the softwood species—cedar, fir, pine, spruce or redwood. Most lumberyards and building supply houses carry wood species from nearby lumbering regions. They are usually more economical than species shipped in from distant areas, but any species of lumber may be special ordered.

Pressure-treated lumber is rapidly replacing the traditional, naturally decay-resistant species for outdoor construction because it is a better value. Pressure-treated lumber will last outdoors for 40 to 50 years.

Naturally decay-resistant wood species—red cedar, redwood or cypress—will rot in damp locations in 8 to 10 years.

Naturally decay-resistant wood usually comes from the heartwood or center of the tree. If wood will be in contact with the ground or concrete, it should be treated with chemical preservatives.

Pressure-treated wood has preservatives forced deep into its cells to make it resistant to decay, insects, weather and fire. The wood weathers to a silver-gray color similar to the color of untreated woods, but it looks different when new. It typically has a greenish cast.

Pressure-treated woods need no further treatment except in cases where cut ends will come in contact with paving or soil. Use wood preservatives to treat cut ends in such cases. See page 158 for more information on chemical preservatives for wood products.

The choice of lumber for your fence, gate or wall depends on your design, the climate and amount of money you want to spend.

Properly stacked and stored, lumber will be free of warps and other defects that may occur after it is graded. Grapestakes, in the foreground, are a rustic, fence-siding material of redwood or cedar. Grapestakes are derived from a type of stake used in California vineyards.

Cut ends of lumber stack create interesting patterns and textures in late afternoon sun. Natural beauty and strength of wood make it an attractive fencing material.

Lumber Classifications

Use Classifications—This classification is based on descriptions of the way lumber will be used. Classes include yard lumber, structural lumber or shop lumber.

Yard Lumber includes those grades, patterns and sizes that are generally intended for ordinary construction and general building purposes. This category includes framing lumber, studs, plates, rafters and joints. Most fence lumber is included in this classification.

Structural Lumber is larger stock. It is used where structural stresses are required. It is 2 inches or more in *nominal* thickness and width. Nominal refers to the size of a piece of lumber before it is *dressed* and seasoned. Dressed lumber has been smoothed on all sides.

Factory And Shop Lumber is produced or selected primarily for *remanufacturing* purposes. Remanufacturing of lumber involves cutting larger pieces into several different smaller sizes as needed.

Manufacturing Classifications—This refers to the extent that lumber has been *finished*. Finishing involves cutting boards to width and thickness and surfacing the sides and edges by *planing* or sanding. Planing removes a thin layer of wood on each side or edge. A high-speed machine, called a planer, uses a series of sharp, revolv-

Dressed lumber is smooth on all four sides. Each surface and both edges are planed and jointed to produce a board uniform in width and thickness.

ing blades to remove the wood. There are six basic manufacturing classifications.

Dressed Lumber is planed or sanded to ensure smoothness of all surfaces and uniform sizing. Planing is sometimes called *surfacing.*

Dressed lumber is useful for gates because of the finished appearance. It has less tendency to splinter and is preferred as fence siding for dressy-looking designs.

Dressing or planing of lumber is described as follows.
- Surfaced on one side—S1S
- Surfaced on two sides—S2S
- Surfaced on four sides—S4S
- Surfaced on one edge—S1E
- Surfaced on two edges—S2E

Matched Lumber is cut with a tongue on one edge and a groove on the other edge. Tongue-and-groove lumber forms a close, tight joint when two boards are fitted together. If the ends of the boards are also tongue-and-groove, the lumber is referred to as *end-notched.*

Shiplapped Lumber has been cut with a *rabbet joint* on each edge to provide a close, overlapped joint when two pieces are fitted together. A rabbet joint removes 1/2 the thickness of a piece of lumber to a uniform depth along the edge of a board. This forms a lip.

Rough-Sawn Lumber is sawed, edged and trimmed on four surfaces. It has not been dressed or surface-planed to produce a finished surface. The saw marks will still show on all four surfaces. It is an excellent, economical choice for low retaining walls, fenceposts and rails. Rough-sawn boards are good for siding on rustic-looking fence designs.

Economy often dictates the choice of lumber used. Because the back side of fence boards and butted-together edges are usually not seen, S1S boards can produce a finished appearance. It is not economical to use redwood for a fence that will be painted. Pressure-treated fir will last longer, give the same finished appearance after painting and be more economical.

Rough-sawn lumber is sawed, edged and trimmed on all four surfaces. It has not been dressed or planed. Saw marks are clearly visible.

Lumber Grades

Lumber is graded by regional associations of softwood manufacturers. Each association establishes the grading rules for the species of lumber produced by its members. These inspections are based on strict rules set forth by the U.S. Department of Commerce.

Lumber is graded by appearance, strength and utility. The grading rules establish ranges of acceptable defects.

The basic grade classifications for lumber are outlined in the chart below. For economy, choose the lowest grade that will be adequate for your design. Do not buy inferior materials, but it is not necessary to use expensive grades of lumber.

Lumber may not always be properly stacked and stored. This results in warping and decay of the lumber. If you place an order and lumber arrives in poor condition, refuse the delivery.

Kiln-dried lumber is preshrunk in special ovens to remove moisture. It is expensive but worth the cost for detailing of fences and screens or for carpentry work on gates. This lumber will not shrink after a project is completed.

SOFTWOODS

Species include fir, pine, spruce, cedar and cypress.

SELECT—Highest quality lumber used for indoor furnishings, cabinets, trims or high strength.

Grade	Use
A	Practically clear wood. Used for finest construction.
B	A few small imperfections. Appearance is smooth and fine. General and cabinet use.
C	Limited number of small defects covered easily by paint. General use.
D	Small, tight knots easily covered by paint.

COMMON—General garden construction lumber. Boards contain defects that detract from appearance.

Grade	Use
No. 1	Best appearance. Small, tight knots, warp-free. Used for siding, shelving, paneling and high-quality construction.
No. 2	Loose knots, checks and discoloration are acceptable. General use, fencing.
No. 3	Contains large, coarse knots and small knotholes, checks and pitch. May be warped. Useful for fence boards, general construction.
No. 4	Many knotholes, blemishes, splits. Low-quality but low-cost. For rustic fencing.
No. 5	Inferior. Unacceptable for use.

DIMENSION—Structural and engineering uses; posts and beams graded according to strength. For stud walls, plates, sills, cripples, blocking.

Grade	Use
Construction	Good-quality structural grade. Few defects or irregularities.
Standard	More defects than construction, but same strength.
Utility	Not used for fencing or structural uses without additional support. Inferior.
Economy	Inferior quality. Acceptable for temporary bracing.

REDWOOD

Species are naturally decay resistant. *Heart* refers to heartwood.

Grade	Use
Clear	All-heart, finest quality. Knot-free for tight joinery, architectural and decorative uses.
Clear	Fine quality. Small knots, minor blemishes. Tight joinery and architectural uses.
Select Heart	All heart with slight defects. Small, tight knots, torn grain. High strength.
Construction Heart	Contains some large, tight knots. General purpose for posts and deck structures.
Select	Few imperfections, but not as decay resistant as heart grades.
Construction Common	Recommended for fencing and deck boards, all-purpose construction. Contains tight knots, some sapwood and discoloration.
Merchantable	Economical fencing and deck boards. Select with care to avoid loose knots and knotholes. Contains both heart and sapwood.

PLYWOOD

Layers of thin wood veneers laminated together under pressure and heat. Used for interior and exterior construction.

Grade	Use
A-A Exterior	Premier quality. Use where fine appearance on both sides is desirable. Sanded smooth, easy to paint or finish.
A-B Exterior	One side is premier quality. Back side is nice but may have some tight knots. Sanded smooth, easy to paint or finish.
A-C Exterior	One side premier quality. Back side has tight knots, knotholes and minor defects.
B-B Exterior	Both sides reasonably smooth. Utility uses where fine appearance is not essential. Easy to paint or finish.
B-C Exterior	One side reasonably smooth. Some splits and knotholes on the back. Utility use.
C-C Exterior	Rough and difficult to paint. Use where surface will be covered or appearance is not essential.

Lumber Defects

The natural characteristics of wood develop as a tree grows. When a tree is milled for lumber, these characteristics appear as defects in the surface. Defects are also caused by milling errors or shipping damage. Defects can affect the strength and appearance of lumber. Become familiar with the common defects shown below. If defects are minor, you can often save money by using lower grade lumber.

Lumber has defects such as knots, checks, warps, splits and cups. See the photographs and descriptions below. No piece is perfect. The more blemish-free the lumber, the more it costs.

Purchasing lumber by grade gives you a good idea of the quality of the lumber. Selecting individual boards at a lumberyard requires time and patience for sorting through stacks of lumber. Hand selection ensures you'll get the best boards in that grade of lumber. Take special care when choosing pieces for detailed fences, gates and screens.

Wear gloves to avoid splinters. Look for lumber with straight-grain patterns. Avoid pieces with decay, pitch or sap. Don't select boards that are warped or twisted. Loose knots are not a problem except near cuts. Knots can be popped and glued back in place. Straighten piles of lumber when you leave the lumberyard.

Shake—A separation along the grains of a piece of lumber. Usually occurs between the rings of annual growth.

Twist—Deviation from the flat planes of all four faces. Caused by a spiraling or twisting action. Usually caused by seasoning or aging.

White Speck Or Honeycomb—Caused by a fungus in the living tree. White speck is small white pits or spots. Honeycomb is similar, but its pits are larger or deeper.

Wane—The presence of bark or lack of wood on the edge or corner of a piece of lumber. This is a visual defect.

Split—Similar to checks, except separation of wood fibers extends through a piece of lumber. Usually occurs at ends of boards.

Knots—May be solid, loose or missing. Missing knots leave a knothole. Knots may appear on one or more faces of a board. Solid knots do not affect strength.

Crook—Deviation from a flat plane of the narrow face of a board. Occurs from end to end.

Bow—Distortion in a board where the deviation from flatness is lengthwise along the board. Does not occur across the face.

Decay—A disintegration of the wood due to wood-destroying fungi. These fungi require a wet environment in which to grow.

Lumber Sizes

Size classifications are used to designate all lumber. Lumber in these classifications is usually common grade. See page 55 for an explanation of grades of lumber.

Boards—Lumber that is less than 2 inches thick and 2 inches or more wide. Boards less than 6 inches wide may be called *strips*.

Dimension—Boards that are at least 2 inches thick and up to 5 inches wide. Dimension lumber may be called *framing, joists, planks, rafters, studs* or *small timbers*.

Timber—Lumber that is 5 inches or more at its smallest dimension. Timber may be called *beams, posts, stringers, caps, sills* or *girders*.

Lumber comes in all sizes and lengths in 2-foot increments. When planning your fence or wall design, use even lengths of lumber for efficiency and economy. Determine every piece you will need to construct the project and list all items exactly. Give the exact dimension for lengths.

Nominal sizes are used when purchasing all lumber. Exact dimensions are given for length. Nominal size refers to the size, width and thickness of a piece of lumber before it is dressed and planed. It is commonly used to designate a particular size piece of lumber—2x4, 2x6 and so on. The nominal size is larger than the actual size of a piece of lumber.

Actual size is the minimum size of a board after it is dressed and planed. A nominal 2x4 measures 1-1/2x3-1/2". See chart at right.

SIZES OF LUMBER

Terms used to designate sizes of lumber are nominal dimensions. The actual size is smaller. Actual sizes are exact, but nominal sizes are used when purchasing lumber.

"Two-by" or greater size lumber is approximately 1/2 inch smaller than its nominal size. "One-by" or smaller size lumber is approximately 1/4 inch smaller than its nominal size.

This chart shows size differences between nominal and actual size.

Nominal Size (inches)	Actual Dry Size (inches)
1x2	3/4x1-1/2
1x4	3/4x3-1/2
1x6	3/4x5-1/2
2x4	1-1/2x3-1/2
4x4	3-1/2x3-1/2
4x6	3-1/2x5-1/2
6x6	5-1/2x5-1/2

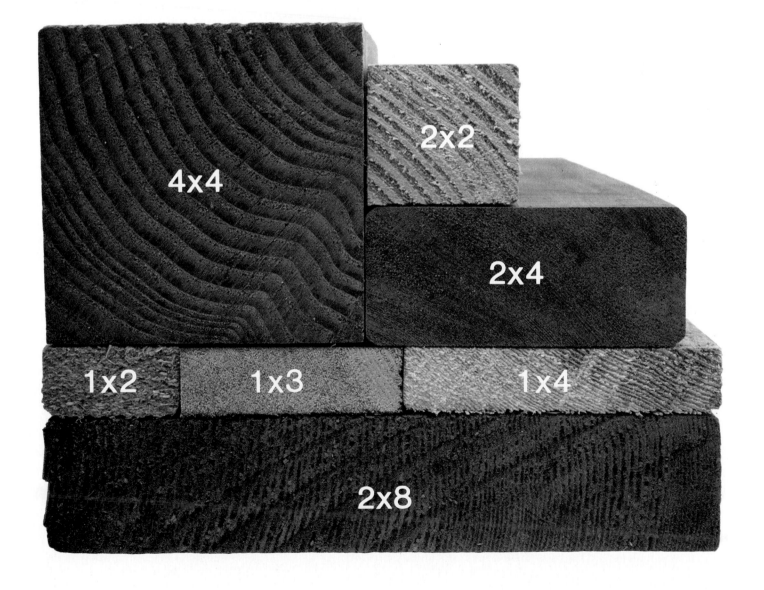

Solid-board siding fence is economical and easy to build.

Traditional ball-style finial tops a post. Finials are available prefabricated.

Plywood-siding fence with contrasting wood cap.

Fencing Lumber

The following list describes some of the more common types of wooden fencing materials available at lumberyards and home centers. Because of regional variations, some types may not be available throughout the country.

Board Siding—Available with plain or tongue-and-groove edges. Board siding produces solid fences with no gaps between boards. Thin strips of wood are often nailed over board edges for board-and-batten fencing.

Palings And Poles—Wood stakes 2 to 12 inches in diameter with pointed tops. They are usually rough saplings stripped of bark and branches. Palings are turned on a lathe to obtain a smooth surface. Palings are small-diameter poles used for stockade-style fencing.

Pressure-treated poles 6 inches in diameter make useful posts for rustic fences.

Plywood—Available in sheets 4 feet wide by 8, 10 or 12 feet long. Plywood is suitable for outdoor projects if it is exterior grade. The thickness for fencing is usually 3/8, 1/2, 5/8 or 3/4 inch. See page 55 for more information on plywood.

Precut Fencing—Lumber presized and cut for posts, rails and board

Palings made from peeled saplings make a solid, stockade-style fence.

Grapestake fence and wood posts support an arbor, screen neighbors and create an outdoor hallway. The hallway leads to a guest house.

Lattice shutters in this fence are opened for a view outside, or closed for complete privacy.

Precut fencing lumber is available in lengths from 2 to 14 feet.

siding. It is available in many do-it-yourself supply centers. There is little margin for measurement error with precut lumber.

Precut Pickets—Fence boards often available in simple picket top styles for use in fences.

Prefabricated Finials—Ornaments for topping posts. They are usually made of hemlock or Douglas fir. Finials are available in many classic styles.

Redwood Grapestakes—Popularly used as fence siding in the western United States. The common grapestake used for fencing is a 1x2" slat, sometimes with one smooth side. It is usually 3 to 6 feet long.

Reed Or Bamboo Fencing—This fencing is manufactured in a similar way to grapestakes, but it has a more attractive appearance.

Shingles, Shakes And Split-Shakes—Usually made of cedar or redwood. They are used for roofing and siding.

Split Rails—Used for post-and-rail fencing and other rustic styles. They measure 5 inches by 6 inches by 8 feet.

Standard Garden Lath—Used for lattice or inserting into chain-link fencing. It is 1/4 inch thick by 1-1/2 inches wide.

Utility Fencing—Comes in large rolls of wooden slats wired together.

Reed or bamboo fencing is an inexpensive temporary screening material.

This 5-rail, zig-zag fence adds a rustic look to this large landscape.

Dark-stained cap and plant material complement simple shingle fence.

Elaborate, notched, spearhead pickets are spaced one picket apart. Use extra picket as a spacer.

This natural-wood fence steps to accommodate the slope. Cap is mitered and overhangs fence at end. Lattice panels were constructed last. Cut several lath pieces on miter box. Use extra strips of lath for spacing. Lay lath in position and attach with nails. Nail every other strip. Do not nail spacers. Cut and attach lath trim strips, mitering the corners. Place all lath in the same plane in the same direction.

This natural-wood lattice fence creates a warm, open feeling in the garden.

Classic Fence Designs

A few classic fence designs are presented on the following pages. Each fence uses the same basic framework with variations in size and design.

LATTICE AND SOLID-BOARD FENCE

The fence shown at top left combines diagonally woven latticework with simple, vertical boards. It requires more time to build than simple fences, but is sturdy and solid. The latticework makes the fence appear to be light and open. Climbing vines can be trained to grow up the fence. The design looks good in both traditional and contemporary settings.

The fence is attractive and neat-looking from either side. It can be painted or left unfinished. The fence can also be stepped down on gently sloping sites.

Materials include 4x4 posts, 2x4 rails, a 2x6 cap with rounded edges, 1x6 vertical boards, 1x2 garden lath and nails. The height of posts and vertical boards and length of rails and cap can be extended or shortened as necessary.

LATTICE FENCE

Attractive details and natural wood combine to create the graceful lattice fence shown at bottom left. This open fence solves the problems of enclosure and boundary definition. Views are minimized without becoming obscured.

The open latticework allows sunlight and breezes to enter. This fence steps down a gentle slope. The same fence could be used effectively on a flat site.

To increase privacy, plant shrubs behind the fence. Vines planted on the fence will create an open and closed effect. Vines must be regularly pruned to reduce weight.

SOLID-BOARD FENCE

Solid-board fences offer complete privacy and create a barrier that prevents breezes from passing through. Solid fences must be built strong to withstand wind. Posts should be set in concrete collars to provide additional strength. Set posts extra-deep if windy conditions are common.

Solid fences are relatively ineffective in protecting large outdoor areas from wind. Wind tends to swirl over the fence top, creating turbulence. The area immediately adjacent to the fence is protected but not the area a short distance away. Small gaps or openings between boards filter wind, break its force and reduce turbulence.

Vertical boards make a long fence appear shorter and taller. Horizontal boards visually stretch a small area and make tall fences appear shorter. Posts are usually spaced 6 feet apart to support horizontal siding. Diagonal boards create a strong visual contrast in the garden.

Alternating panels or *good-neighbor fences* look the same on both sides. They are useful when you and your neighbor are sharing fence costs. Add a decorative cap or battens to create interesting shadow lines on the fence.

Gaps often appear between boards because wood shrinks with age and exposure to weather. These gaps can be avoided by using tongue-and-groove panels or board battens nailed over gaps.

Decorative cap on this solid-board fence was created by extension of posts and 2x4s above fence siding.

A *good-neighbor fence* looks the same on both sides. Siding for this fence was nailed to oversize rails to create panels. Panels were nailed to posts. Fence is stained.

Flat pickets are placed between rails and chamfered trim pieces to improve appearance of this fence. Pickets wrap around corner posts. Posts do not extend above top rail.

Simple, round-top pickets are spaced one picket apart.

Many styles of pickets are available precut. You can even create your own design.

Elaborate picket pattern gives a Gothic look to this fence. Post top is chamfered to shed water.

PICKET FENCE

The picket fence is quick and easy to build using basic fence construction techniques. The crisp, neat qualities of this traditional design look good with many styles of architecture. The fence goes well with Victorian, Colonial, Cape Cod and ranch-style homes.

A picket fence can unify a large property or enclose a small yard. Its limited height and openness allow views both in and out of the garden.

Planting shrubs next to the fence will provide more privacy. Climbing roses and other vines can be grown against pickets, but plants require pruning when repainting the fence.

Variables to consider in designing a picket fence include length and width of pickets, spacing between pickets, top designs and post ornaments. Alternating picket length or width introduces variety into the pattern.

Attach pickets to the basic framework using the method described on page 47. This produces evenly spaced pickets. Keep bottom ends of pickets at least 2 inches above ground.

Many picket-fence components are available precut and ready to assemble. It is better to buy pickets precut instead of cutting them yourself. You can have pickets custom-milled if a specific design is not commercially available. If you are using an unusual top design, it is best to buy several extra pickets in case replacements are needed in the future.

Pickets are available in lengths of 2 to 5 feet and widths of 2 to 6 inches. Lengths of 2x2s can be substituted for pickets. Decorative post tops, called *finials,* are manufactured to fit standard 4x4 or 6x6 posts.

Prefabricated panels of picket fencing are available. They are convenient to use where there is a gentle slope. Wired-picket utility or snow fencing on a roll is another option. This can be used as a temporary fence.

There are several disadvantages to picket fences. The repetitive design may be monotonous if used in a long, uninterrupted stretch. The design variables previously mentioned can be used to avoid this problem.

The fence offers little resistance to trespassers. Children can easily climb over it. Animals can jump it or dig a hole beneath it. A combination of barrier plantings and a baseboard attached below the pickets can eliminate some of these problems.

Periodic repainting or whitewashing will be necessary unless the fence is left natural.

Below: Square 2x2 pickets of two lengths have pointed tops. Tops complement finials that cap extended post tops. Kickboard nailed to bottom rail and posts discourages animals from digging under fence.

Spring flowers and white pickets are a favorite traditional combination. Pickets define yard without producing a closed-in feeling.

Cedar shingle fence makes a wall-like extension of shingled house walls.

SHINGLE FENCE
The shingle fence is a natural for shingle houses. This fence looks good with other materials too. The shingle fence offers complete privacy. It can enclose a small garden or be used as a wall-like extension of the house. It also makes an excellent background for vines or espaliers.

Because the fence is solid, it blocks light and wind. It must be sturdily built to withstand strong wind. A solid backing is required to attach the shingles with nails or staples.

The basic fence framework of posts and rails is supplemented by a 3/4-inch-thick cap and 3/4-inch plywood sheathing. Shingles are attached to the sheathing.

Start at the bottom and nail a row of shingles on the sheathing. Use a chalkline or line level to mark the horizontal position for the first row of shingles. Chalk more lines up the wall, 6 inches apart to allow a 6-inch exposure of the bottom row. Continue attaching rows of shingles up the wall. The final course of shingles should be approximately 6 inches long.

You can convert an existing board fence to a shingle fence. Follow the procedures described above and attach shingles over existing fence siding. Make sure the nail or staple is short enough so it does not come through the other side of the fence.

FENCE AND ARBOR
This simple design incorporates basic elements of both a fence and *arbor.* An arbor is an overhead structure on which trees or vines are trained to provide shade. The elegant and economical structure shown at left provides privacy for the owners. The fence portion screens the garden from adjacent yards and the street. The arbor conceals the garden from the view of high windows in neighboring buildings.

Climbing vines with hanging fruits and flowers are trained along the arbor. These vines create a living ceiling around the edges of the garden. The arbor is especially attractive and useful for shading outdoor areas. Plants can be hung from projecting supports of the arbor.

Fence-and-arbor combination is creative modification of basic fence. Posts extend up to support small arbor.

SLAT FENCE

The intricate slat fence in the top right photograph encloses an Oriental courtyard and creates a sense of privacy from the street. The basic post-and-rail framework is changed by the arrangement of alternating slats and addition of a cap piece. A middle rail, visible through spaced slats, breaks up the vertical aspect of slats and posts.

Light can shine through the delicate framework and breezes enter through open slats. This fence is appropriate for a small-scale garden.

The redwood fence has been allowed to weather naturally. Redwood's warmth and texture complement the simplicity and sparse detail of the design. Shrubs and trees adjacent to the fence create privacy and vary patterns of light along the fence.

WELDED-WIRE FENCE

Welded-wire fencing is useful where security and visual openness are desired. This fence is simple and inexpensive. It creates an effective barrier to intruders and makes a suitable enclosure for animals, children or a swimming pool area.

A wire fence serves as a ready-made trellis. Plant vines at the bottom to produce a living fence in a short time. This type of fence also helps support hedges and keeps them straight.

Welded-wire fence is strong, durable and easy to maintain. It is usually sold in 50-foot rolls and is available in different mesh sizes, including 1/2x1/2", 1x1", 2x2-1/2" and 2x4". Vinyl-covered and looped, welded-wire varieties are available for decorative looks. Galvanized steel is rust-resistant.

The fence shown at right uses a 2x4" welded-wire mesh, 4x4 posts and 2x4 rails. The easiest way to assemble the fence is to set posts and build the frame first. Then attach wire to the side of the frame.

Wire should be stretched before securing it in place with wire staples. For information on stretching wire, see page 47. Wire is stretched properly when the *tension curves* are about 1/2 to 2/3 their original depth and the wire is springy to the touch. Tension curves are small crimps or bends placed in wire fencing to permit expansion and contraction as temperatures change.

Use staples of the same or heavier weight than the wire. Place the 2-inch dimension of the wire opening horizontally to discourage climbers.

Cover wire edges with a wooden trim piece if you want a more finished appearance. You can also install the wire inside the frame. Use plenty of staples to attach stretched wire to avoid sags and bulges.

New entry gate and fence are detailed to blend together when gate is closed.

Welded-wire fence made from 2x4" wire mesh is attached to decorative wooden frame. This style of fence provides boundary protection for children, pets or a garden area. Wire can serve as a ready-made trellis for vines.

Short fence on brick wall steps to accommodate slope and building-code-imposed fence height. Painted post anchors are set in masonry joints. Brick wall is running-bond pattern with rowlock cap.

FENCE-WALL COMBINATION

In locations where a solid wall would be too massive or expensive and a fence too light, consider building a fence and wall combination. If the wall portion serves as a retaining wall, different levels can be created in the garden.

In the example at left, the fence-wall combination creates a boundary between the driveway parking area and private, sunken courtyard. The good-neighbor fence design is attractive from both sides. The fence top steps down with the stepped wall.

Painted steel post anchors are placed in mortar joints between bricks in the garden wall. Fenceposts are bolted to anchors. Substitute this procedure for basic fence building steps 2 through 5. Fence construction proceeds after posts are in place.

The bottom of the fence should clear the wall by at least 1/2 inch to avoid contact with standing water. The wooden fence is not treated with preservatives because it is not underground. See Chapter 3, page 94, for information on building brick walls.

PLASTIC SCREENS

Acrylic, polyvinyl-chloride and fiber-glass plastic sheets are versatile materials for enclosing gardens. Panels are easily placed inside a wooden frame fence. Plastic sheets are available in many colors and degrees of opaqueness or transparency. Light colors are the most reflective. Obscure, translucent plastic screens reduce glare and allow light to pass through, yet ensure privacy. Plastic sheets are an inexpensive way to screen service areas or other objectionable views.

Most plastics are impervious to weather in terms of strength and endurance, but not finish. Plastics are easily scratched. Plastics are also subject to expansion and contraction because of weather conditions. They may warp and stretch. Use exterior-grade plastic panels designated for garden use.

Install plastic screens so they can be removed when damaged or worn out. It's best to attach the screen to a grid to reduce the panel size. Don't attempt to cover too large an opening, especially in areas of strong wind. Cut plastics with a fine-tooth handsaw, portable electric sabre saw or reciprocating saw.

Plastic panels attached to wooden framework admit light and control wind. Delicate wood framework creates interesting pattern in sunlight.

Plastic panels can be attached to wooden frames by using aluminum-twist nails with a neoprene washer. Space nails 1 foot apart. Predrill nail holes in the sheeting. Make holes slightly larger than the nails. This allows room for expansion and contraction of the plastic, without causing cracks.

If corrugated panels are used, drive the nails through crowns, not valleys. Finish the screen with wooden molding.

Panels can also be slid into grooves cut in wood frames.

GLASS SCREEN

A glass screen can preserve a view or create a room outdoors. There are several pros and cons to using glass for outdoor screens. Glass is a fragile material that requires careful handling and expert installation. The framework to hold a glass screen must be strong. Materials are expensive and are vulnerable to vandalism or accidental breakage.

A clear-glass windscreen that takes advantage of a view provides little privacy. Activities may be in full view of neighbors or the casual passerby.

Glass screens must be supported by strong foundations. A low masonry wall or concrete foundation is recommended. A framework of steel or kiln-dried wood should be used to hold glass. Steel resists warping and has a more delicate appearance than wood. Kiln-dried wood must be painted or sealed to resist warping.

Use standard glass sizes to keep the screen economical and practical. A screen with small glass panes will be stronger than a screen with large panes. Smaller panes require a less-substantial framework. It is also less costly to replace smaller panes if broken. The strength of the glass must be heavy enough to withstand wind and an occasional bird collision.

Glass is available in different strengths and thicknesses. Safety glazing is recommended for any outside application. Tempered and laminated glass is strong, but more expensive than other types. Wire-glass has a wire mesh embedded to reduce the chances of shattering. Blue-glass reduces glare and preserves the view. If privacy is a consideration, use textured, patterned or frosted glass. Heat-absorbing glass is useful for cool-season areas, but it is expensive.

Glass screen wraps around the deck and creates a warm microclimate for succulents and citrus plants.

CANVAS SCREENING

Canvas screens are casual and fresh-looking. They provide privacy and are perfect for beach houses, a swimming pool changing area, or on a balcony or patio in the city. Canvas is durable and easy to replace. Bright or subdued colors of canvas screens can change the mood of a garden.

Canvas screens are effective wind deflectors. They allow a small amount of wind to pass around the edges of the canvas.

To make a canvas fence or screen, first construct a standard wooden fence frame. Then make canvas panels to fit inside the frame. See directions below for sewing canvas. Canvas panels should be slightly smaller than the frame. The edges of the canvas panel should have a metal grommet placed every 8 inches along each edge and in each corner.

Finished panels can be sewn in place using nylon or polyethylene rope. Lace the rope through metal grommets and tie to the fence frame. You can use a combination of metal eye-hooks and grommets. Hold the panel up to the frame and mark grommet locations. Screw in eye-hooks at these locations and stretch canvas over the hooks. Squeeze the hooks together to secure the canvas panels.

Sewing Canvas—Canvas can be sewn by hand, but it is easier to sew with a machine. Heavyweight, 10-ounce

Grommeting canvas is similar to making giant shoelace eyes.

Fasten canvas panels overhead for shade or to upright frames for privacy.

duck or vinyl-coated canvas should be hemmed at an awning shop. If hand-sewing 10-ounce canvas, use a No. 13 sailmaker's needle and dacron thread. Grommets can be installed at an awning shop, or by renting grommet-setting equipment, available in fabric or awning stores.

Trees in the fenceline create special problems. Here a fence jogs around a tree to continue privacy screening. Both fence sections must be on your property for this solution, unless you have a written agreement with your neighbor.

Special Fence Problems

When planning a fence, consider the following potential problems and how they may affect design and location.

Legal Requirements—Local building codes impose restrictions on fences in many parts of the country. There are usually limitations on fence height along property lines. Fences may also have to be located a specific distance back from property lines. Be sure to check all local code requirements before building any fence or wall. It's possible to apply for variances or special permits if the proposed design conflicts with codes.

Attractive Nuisance—The law usually requires swimming pools to be fenced because they are considered to be an attractive nuisance. If you have a pool or are planning one, make sure your fence design meets legal requirements for fencing around pools.

Obstructions—There may be obstructions along the location where you plan to put your fence. These obstructions can be above or below ground. Be sure to locate all utility lines that may be in the way. If necessary, check with utility companies before digging postholes. Determine if the obstruction can be removed, relocated or remain in place. Obstructions may require modification of fence design.

Mature trees should be preserved. If a tree is in the way, build the fence around the tree. Build the fence right up to the tree, leaving several inches on either side for the trunk to grow. Keep posts several feet away from the tree to protect root systems. Then build a frame around the tree to support the extended fence. If possible, design the fence so boards can be removed or changed at a later date.

Never use the tree trunk as a fencepost. Driving nails into a tree damages the bark. Damaged tissues and nail holes are invitations to infection.

If you encounter large rocks or boulders partly above ground, adjust the fence section to rise at the bottom. Keep the top of the fence level. Frame around the boards to secure them and prevent warping.

Large boulders below ground are a different problem. If these rocks or boulders are not too large, you can dig them up. Digging them up may be difficult. Boulders are usually much larger than they first appear. The best solution is to relocate postholes.

If there is a gully or ditch the fence must cross, use longer side boards to fill the void below the bottom rail. Do not allow boards to touch the ground.

Slopes—Hilly slopes can create special problems. When fencing along a hillside, step the fence down in level sections or follow the contour of the slope.

If the slope is gentle and gradual, set posts at the same height at regular intervals. Then attach the rails parallel to the incline. Use a carpenter's level to keep posts and boards 90° vertical.

If the ground is uneven or slopes irregularly, keep the top of the fence level and use some posts that are longer than others.

On a steep slope, step the fence down in sections by connecting vertical posts with horizontal rails. You may have to space posts of the same height close together. Use a carpenter's level to keep the fence level and 90° vertical. Where the slope varies, set posts at different heights. Keep rail length consistent.

To determine the method of sloped fencing that looks best, make a sketch showing the fence two ways: stepped and following the slope. See page 71.

Neighbors—Talk to your neighbors when planning a fence or wall. They may be willing to share costs and help do the work. If you agree to place the fence on the property line, document the agreement through written correspondence or an informal contract. A good-neighbor fence looks the same on both sides. The most common way to attach siding to these fences is to nail pieces or blocks of siding to alternate sides of the rails.

If you and your neighbors are unable to agree on fence plans, go ahead and build the fence inside your property line. Check local codes for setback requirements. Make sure you obtain a legal description and survey of your property boundaries.

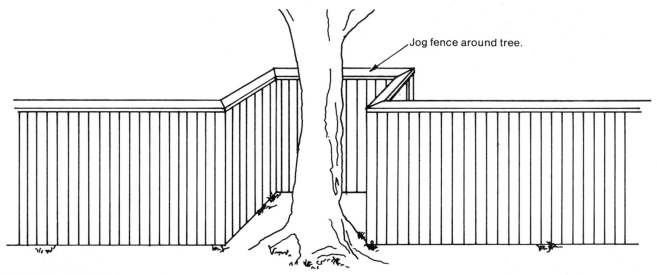

Jog fence around tree.

Tree In Fenceline

Solving the problem of a tree in the fenceline is easy—if the tree is not located on the property line. Jog the fence around the tree. The tree can be included or excluded in the landscape. Avoid damage to tree roots when digging post holes.

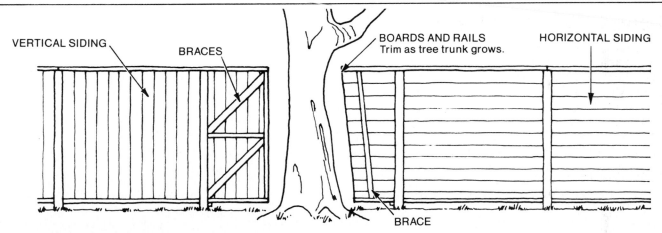

VERTICAL SIDING

BRACES

BOARDS AND RAILS
Trim as tree trunk grows.

HORIZONTAL SIDING

BRACE

Tree On Property Line

Use these two methods when the tree is located on the property line. The idea on the left is for vertical board siding. The one on the right is for horizontal board siding. Post holes are dug away from the tree to prevent root damage. Fence siding is brought close to the tree trunk. Allow some room for tree growth. Bracing is angled up to outside edge of fence sections.

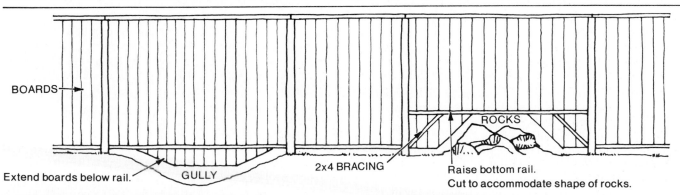

BOARDS

Extend boards below rail.

GULLY

2x4 BRACING

ROCKS

Raise bottom rail.
Cut to accommodate shape of rocks.

Fencing Around Obstructions

When a fence must span a gully, boards can be extended below the bottom rail and cut to follow contours. Leave clearance for drainage water. Fill the space between the gully and fence with wire fencing to keep animals out. To clear a rock outcropping, raise the bottom rail and cut boards to clear the obstruction. Use extra bracing to prevent boards from breaking or warping.

Plotting Slopes

The easiest method for plotting small sloping areas is to place a short stake at the top of the slope. Place a longer stake in level ground at the bottom of the slope. Make sure the top of this stake is *higher* than the stake at the top of the slope.

Stretch a string from the base of the top stake to near the top of the second one. Using a line level, adjust the string end up or down on the tall stake until the string is level.

Measure the distance from the string at the top of the long stake to the ground. This is the *rise* or vertical difference. The distance between the two stakes along the string is the *run*.

It is easy to plot a slope on graph paper by making each square equal 1 foot. Count up for rise and across for run, then connect the two end points with a diagonal line. Use this sketch for planning. Overlay tracing paper and experiment with various designs.

A more practical method for large areas requires two people and a special tool—a hand level or surveyor's transit. Sight from a fixed eyelevel point to a tape measure or surveyor's rod. The difference in grade between the two points is then determined and plotted on paper. This process is repeated for many points on the site.

The points on paper are connected by contours. The result is a map or grading plan. It may be easier to mark grade changes on the ground with stakes and lay out the proposed design with strings.

Sloping sites create special fence problems. Stepping a fence down a slope in increments is one solution. Step rails down a minimum of 3 inches, even if slope is gradual.

PLOTTING SLOPES

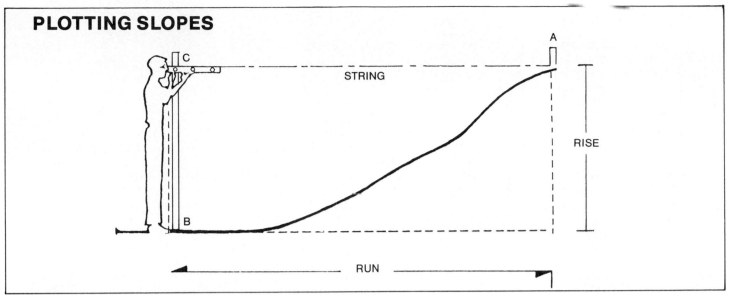

Plotting the rise and run on sloping ground is not difficult. It does require careful measurements. Use the following method to find the rise and run of any slope. Drive a stake at the highest point on the slope, point A. Drive a long stake at the lowest point on the slope, point B. Make sure the top of this stake is higher than the bottom of the stake at point A. Position a level or hand level on the long stake approximately at point C. Sight along the level to the stake at point A. Move the level up and down on the long stake until it indicates level with the stake at point A. Mark point C on the long stake where level is indicated. Measure the distance between point C and the ground. This distance is the amount of rise, or vertical distance, of the slope. Attach a string between point C to the stake at point A. Measure this distance. This measurement is the run of the slope.

SLOPED FENCE

STEPPED FENCE

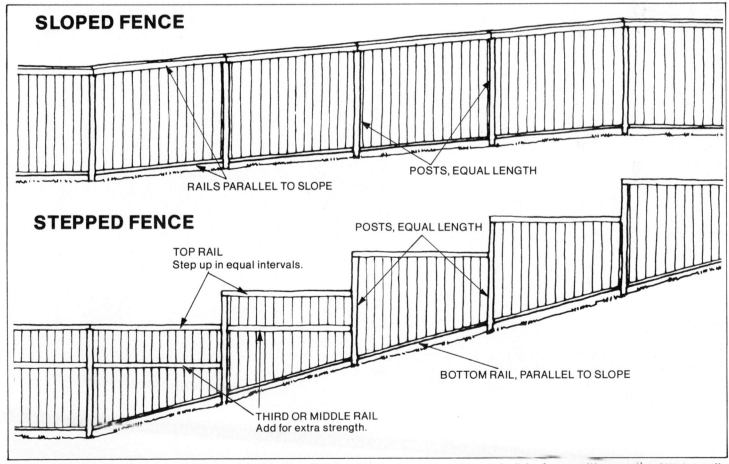

Building fences on slopes requires careful planning. The top illustration shows how to build a fence with a continuous top rail. The top and bottom of the fence are parallel to the ground slope. All posts are the same height. The bottom illustration shows a fence built in stepping sections. The top rail of each fence section is horizontally level. The bottom rail of the fence is parallel to the slope. Posts are the same height. The length of each fence section may be adjusted to accommodate the grade of the slope.

3

HOW TO BUILD WALLS

This chapter describes several basic wall-construction methods. Several outstanding wall designs are shown. Each wall is unique, but all the designs shown contain the same basic elements. Use these designs as ideas for building your own wall. You can elaborate on simple designs or modify others to suit your landscape.

Walls can be built in many different designs and kinds of materials. Among the most popular materials are bricks, concrete blocks and native stones. Other materials, such as wooden timbers, railroad ties and even wooden frames with stucco coverings are used to build walls. See page 80 for detailed information on building materials.

Basic Wall Components

Walls have some or all of the following:
- Footing or foundation
- Building units such as masonry, stone, wood or glass block
- Reinforcing materials
- Fastening materials
- Wall caps and veneer coverings
- Hardware and wiring

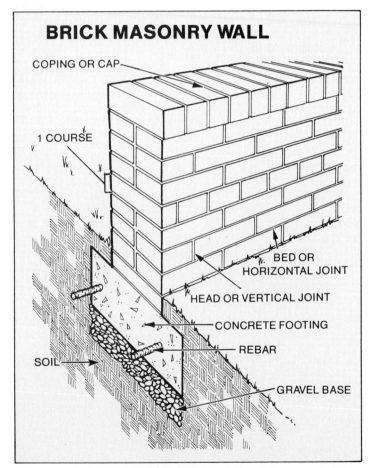

BRICK MASONRY WALL

COPING OR CAP
1 COURSE
BED OR HORIZONTAL JOINT
HEAD OR VERTICAL JOINT
CONCRETE FOOTING
REBAR
SOIL
GRAVEL BASE

Masonry unit walls are built with a reinforced-concrete footing, coursed masonry units of brick, concrete block or stone, and mortar to hold the wall units together.

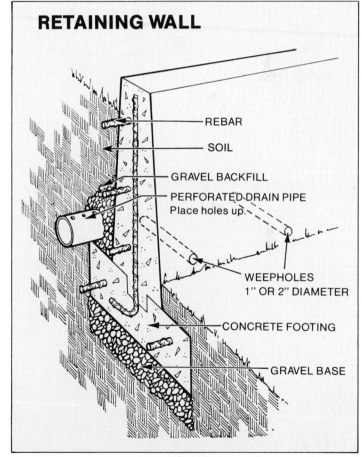

RETAINING WALL

REBAR
SOIL
GRAVEL BACKFILL
PERFORATED DRAIN PIPE
Place holes up.
WEEPHOLES
1" OR 2" DIAMETER
CONCRETE FOOTING
GRAVEL BASE

Components of a poured-concrete retaining wall include a reinforced footing with a keyed joint, a poured-concrete wall with reinforcing rods, gravel backfill, drainage pipe and weepholes for additional water drainage.

Left: Flagstone veneer attached to low, concrete-block wall complements flagstone paving and veneered house wall. Entry is attractive and easy to maintain.

FOOTINGS

Walls must be built on a stable base. The base can be the ground, but most walls require a concrete footing or foundation constructed below ground.

Low garden walls of stone, broken concrete or timber can be built with no footing. The weight and position of materials holds low walls in place. Minor shifting because of soil movement is acceptable. Low masonry walls, 2 feet tall or less, can be built on a simple masonry footing. Tall masonry walls, those over 2 feet tall, require a poured-concrete footing.

Footing Fundamentals

Footing designs vary with size and type of wall. Footing width is usually 2/3 the wall height; for low walls, twice the wall width. Footing depth should equal wall width at base. The chart below gives common footing

Wall Height (H)	Footing Width (W)
1'	8"
2'	16"
3'	24"
4'	32"
5'	40"
6'	48"

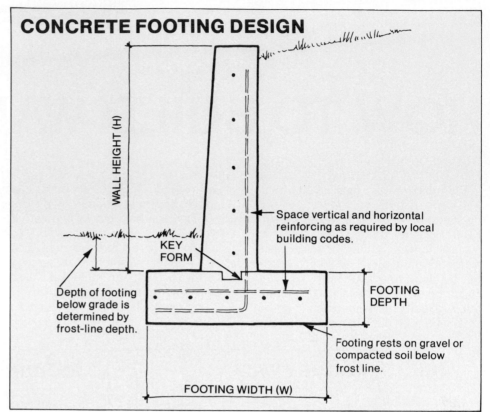

CONCRETE FOOTING DESIGN

WALL HEIGHT (H)

Space vertical and horizontal reinforcing as required by local building codes.

KEY FORM

Depth of footing below grade is determined by frost-line depth.

FOOTING DEPTH

Footing rests on gravel or compacted soil below frost line.

FOOTING WIDTH (W)

For walls over 2 feet, footing width should be 2/3 the wall height. Footing depth should equal wall width, or wall height divided by 12, whichever dimension is greater. Reinforcing should be placed in the footing according to local building-code requirements. Key form helps anchor poured-concrete walls to footing. Do not make a key in the footing if wall will be built of brick or block.

widths. Before pouring footings, consult the building department about the *frost-line depth*. Frost-line depth refers to how deep frost penetrates ground in winter. It is important to know where the frost-line is if you live in a cold climate. The frost-line depth is added to footing depth. Some building codes require special construction methods for footings in regions with frost heaving.

Dig a trench the shape of the footing and slightly deeper than the frost-line depth. Firmly tamp soil in trench bottom and fill with 6 inches of gravel. Place 6 inches of gravel in the trench bottom. The top of the gravel layer must be below the frost line.

If the soil is firm and relatively free of rocks, use the earth itself as the footing form. If the trench walls are too soft or damp to hold a vertical

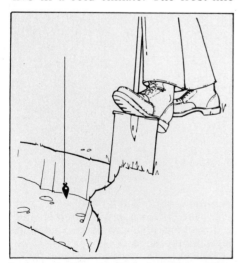

Lay out the footing location using batter boards. Use a straight-bladed shovel to dig footing trench. Keep the sides of the trench vertical. Check depth with a plumb bob.

Compact soil in trench bottom by tamping. Use a rented or homemade tamper. Tamping reduces further settling of the soil.

In areas with poorly drained soil, dig trench deeper and fill with 6 inches of gravel. In areas with a deep frost line, fill most of the trench with gravel.

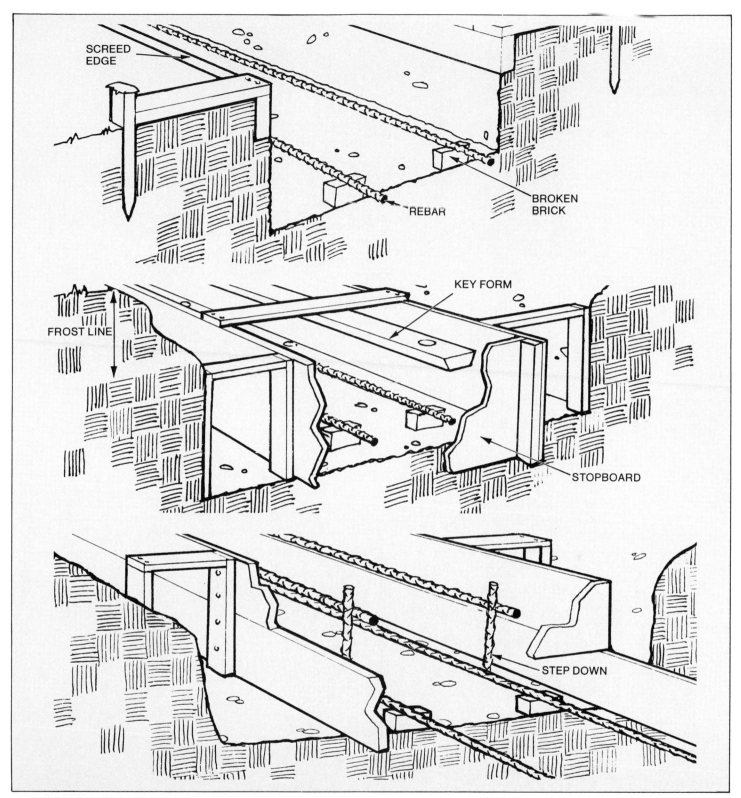

SCREED EDGE

REBAR

BROKEN BRICK

KEY FORM

FROST LINE

STOPBOARD

STEP DOWN

CONSTRUCTING FOOTING FORMS

Construct a footing form using one of the three options shown. Reinforcing should rest on pieces of broken brick, stone or concrete. Place reinforcing rods 1/3 of the way up from trench bottom. Rebar should be at least 1-1/2 inches away from all form boards. Attach vertical rebar with wire. Top: Firm soil and minimal frost-line depth permits use of trench as formwork. Smooth, level footing surface is needed for brick or block walls. Level and brace 2x4s along the trench edge to form a screed edge. Center: Wooden forms are necessary in soils that do not hold a firm edge. This example is built below the frost line. A 2x4 key form has been positioned to make a key in the footing. Holes are placed in the key form for rebar. A concrete wall will be poured after the footing cures. Bottom: This footing steps down a sloping site. Reinforcing also steps down. Rebar is wired in place and does not touch trench bottom, formwork or stopboards. Stepped footings are economical for sloping sites.

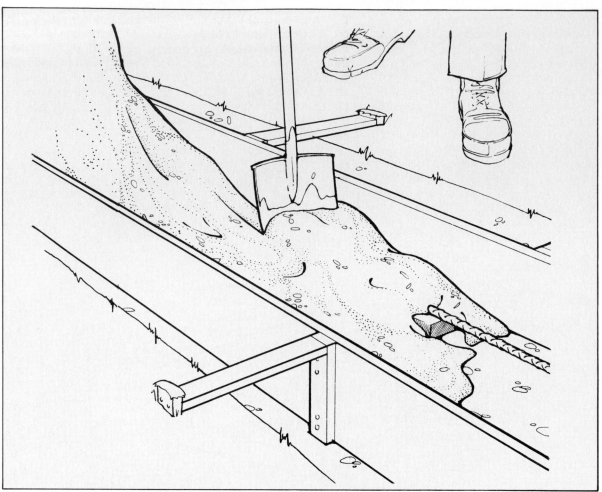

Coat inside of footing form with clean motor oil. Pour concrete in trench and tamp in place. Work from one end of the form to the other. Try to eliminate all voids or air pockets in wet concrete. Stop the pour just short of the form end to allow space for excess concrete from the screeding process.

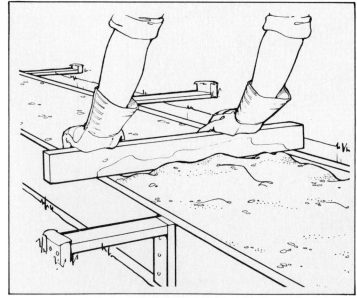

Screed concrete at top of form with scrap of lumber wider than form. Work from one end of the form to the other. Move screed in a zig-zag motion, filling low spots and leveling high spots. If the wall requires steel reinforcing, insert rebar in wet cement. Be sure rebar does not touch the bottom of the trench. If the footing has a key form, remove it as soon as concrete holds its shape.

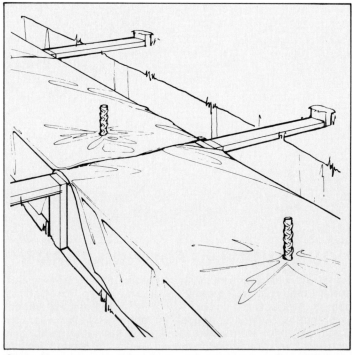

Cover the concrete-filled form with plastic sheeting. Allow the footing to cure for a minimum of four days. Once concrete has cured, remove the forms.

edge, use *spreader forms.*

Spreader forms are used to hold concrete in the shape of the footing. They are made from stock lumber.

Steel reinforcing rods, called *rebars,* should be used for strong footings. See page 152. Place reinforcing rods on small pieces of brick, rock or broken concrete in the footing trench or form. Place the rods 2/3 of the way down from the top of the footing. A 12x12'' concrete footing would have two 1/2-inch reinforcing rods placed 4 inches above *grade.* Grade refers to the bottom of the footing.

After the footing trench has been dug and spreader forms built, the concrete can be poured. You can use premixed, ready-to-pour concrete for large footing areas, or mix your own concrete for smaller areas. See the section on concrete, page 121, to learn how to mix your own concrete or order premixed concrete from local suppliers.

Pour the concrete and screed and smooth the top of the footing. It must be level. The top can remain smooth if a masonry wall will be built.

Poured-concrete walls require a *key* formed in the top. The key is a narrow slot in the top of the footing. The form for making a key must be made when placing footing forms. The key locks the second pour of concrete—the wall—to the footing. See the illustration on page 75 for instructions on how to form a key.

After the footing is poured and smoothed or keyed, allow it to set and *cure* for at least four days. See page 123 for curing procedures.

Curing is a chemical process called *hydration.* Hydration permits the cement in concrete to react with water and harden. Curing requires keeping the concrete footing damp for several days.

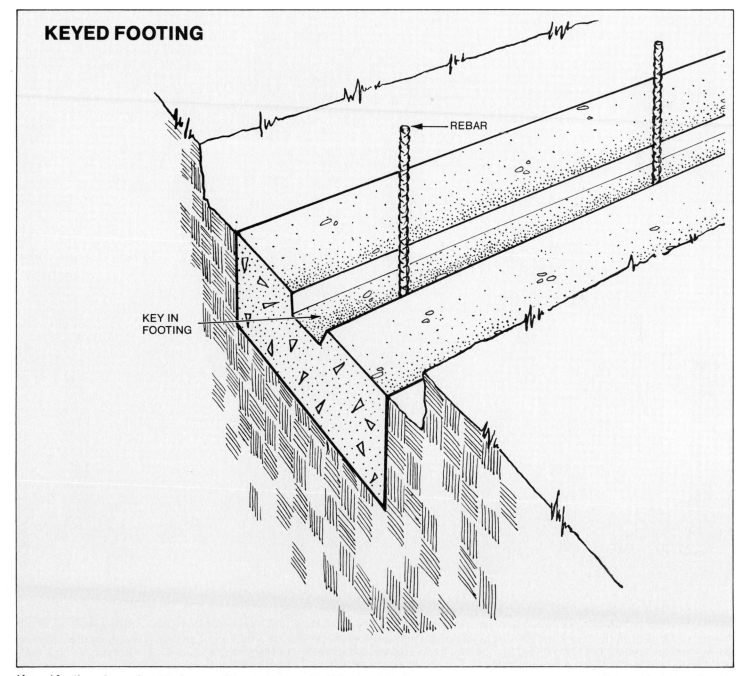

KEYED FOOTING

REBAR

KEY IN FOOTING

Keyed footing shown here helps anchor poured-concrete walls to footings.

Batter Boards

Batter boards mark and hold reference points for building straight walls with square corners. Batter boards also make useful markers for aligning walls or fences. Stakes are easily knocked out of place and chalklines are soon covered by dirt.

Position single batter boards at the open ends of proposed walls. Use double batter boards at corners.

This method uses double batter boards for finding square corners.

1. Drive stakes at the exact locations of outside corners of walls.
2. Drive a small nail into the top of each stake to exactly mark proposed wall corners. The nail indicates this point.
3. Attach heavy twine to all corner nails and extend each line 4 feet beyond each stake. Secure the ends of these lines with additional stakes, forming two sides of a square.
4. Use a carpenter's square to locate a point diagonally opposite the proposed wall corner. This completes the square formed by the line extensions.
5. Drive a stake to mark this new corner point. Drive a nail into the stake and attach the line extensions. Remove the stakes holding the extended lines.
6. From the new corner point, extend the lines another 8 feet. Drive stakes at these two points.
7. Nail an 8-foot-long horizontal board 1 or 2 feet above ground between the corner and one end stake. Level the board.
8. Nail a second horizontal board from the corner to the second end stake. Level the board and place it at the same height as the first board.
9. Support the two end stakes by nailing more boards and stakes as braces.
10. Repeat the entire process for each corner or end of the wall you construct.
11. After all corner batter boards are in position, stretch the strings between the batter boards. You will need a helper. Use a line level to level strings between the batter boards.
12. Hang a lightweight plumb bob at the corner point where strings intersect. It should line up above the nail head on the first stakes.
13. Check for square corners by the 3-4-5 triangulation method. Make a triangle from scrap lumber with a 3-foot side, a 4-foot side and a 5-foot (hypotenuse) side. Check the corner for squareness. If the corner is not square, move the string lines or batter boards until all corners are exactly square.
14. Notch the batter boards to hold the strings in position.

Find a square corner by using the 3-4-5 triangle method. After the first horizontal layout line has been established, locate the perpendicular layout line. Mark 3 feet on one stringline and 4 feet on the other stringline. Adjust one of the layout strings until the diagonal or hypotenuse distance between the points equals 5 feet. The rough perpendicular will become exactly perpendicular and the two lines will form a 90° right angle.

LAYING OUT BATTER BOARDS

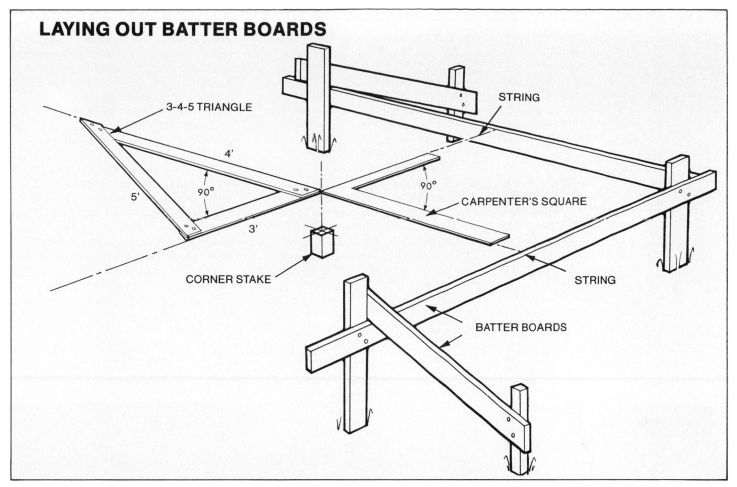

See opposite page for procedure to lay out square corner of wall using batter boards and string.

Use batter boards to hold strings that locate edges of fenceposts and walls. Notch batter boards to hold strings securely.

BUILDING UNITS

Building units are basic materials used to build walls. They include masonry, stone and wood materials.

Masonry—Masonry units are the most popular materials used for walls. Masonry units include adobe, bricks, concrete blocks, poured concrete and glass blocks. Stones or rocks are part of this category.

Work with stone or masonry materials is also called *masonry.* Most walls, except poured-concrete walls, are built in *courses* or horizontal layers of masonry materials. One course of bricks or concrete blocks is one layer of these units. Several courses laid on top of each other form the vertical wall face. The width of a wall is called the *wythe.* A one-wythe wall is one masonry unit wide. A two-wythe wall has two masonry units.

A joint is formed where masonry units are joined. These joints may fit together in several ways. All joints are held together by *mortar.*

Mortar is a mixture of cement or lime, sand and water. Mortar is an adhesive and filler between masonry.

Mortar joints are smoothed and shaped, or *tooled,* to obtain an attractive, watertight surface. See page 103 for specific instructions on how to tool masonry joints.

Some masonry walls are built by the *drywall* method. A drywall is constructed without mortar. The weight of the materials and careful placement keeps drywalls from falling down. This often involves carefully cutting and fitting stones together. It is extremely important to get the base course of a drywall correctly positioned.

Glass Blocks—Glass blocks are grouped with masonry materials. Glass blocks are used to build walls in the same manner as bricks or concrete blocks. Glass blocks are made by fusing two preformed pieces of pressed glass together under heat and pressure. See page 111 for instructions on building a glass-block wall.

Wooden Materials—All kinds of wooden materials can be used to build walls. Large timbers, railroad ties and telephone poles can be placed horizontally or vertically to form freestanding or retaining walls. Wood products can be used in combination with masonry units to construct walls.

Wooden frames made from 2x4s or other stock lumber can be covered with plywood and stucco, wood-shake shingles, or faced with veneers to create walls.

Beautiful red-brick wall and patio reflect warmth of masonry construction. High walls offer privacy and security. Integrated plantings soften wall lines, making this an inviting and relaxing landscape.

Rock wall is laid dry. This primitive type of masonry construction does not use mortar. These types of walls are strong and attractive.

Glass block is a versatile masonry unit material. In this setting, glass-block walls curve around an outdoor-dining area. The block makes an elegant, translucent screen.

A tall poured-concrete or concrete-block wall makes the most effective noise barrier. This poured-concrete wall has a custom-designed, hand-seeded aggregate design.

Retaining walls constructed over 4 feet high must be designed by an engineer to be structurally strong and safe.

FASTENERS

Several kinds of fasteners are used to join building units together. Masonry units use mortar, metal reinforcing and tie bars. Wood units use nails, screws, nuts and bolts, and adhesives.

Here are some common connectors used for fences and walls.

Mortar—Mortar is used to fasten masonry units together. It is made from a mixture of cement or lime, sand and water. Mortar is mixed in small batches so it won't dry and harden before it is used. See page 151 for instructions on mixing mortar.

Anchor Bolts Or J-Bolts—These fasteners are set into wet concrete, *grout* or mortar to hold wooden elements such as sole plates, benches or screen panels. Grout is a thin mortar.

Carriage Bolts—Used with a nut to attach posts to anchors or as a substitute for J-bolts. Carriage bolts are versatile and can be used for many jobs. The square shoulder holds the bolt as the nut is tightened. Use a washer with the nut for greater strength.

Mud Sill Anchors—These anchors are used for connecting stud wall sill plates to wet concrete or masonry joints. The anchors are nailed to the wood sill and then set into wet concrete or mortar.

Masonry Ties—Ties are used to hold two wythes of masonry together. Some ties are used for holding veneer facing to walls. Ties can be inserted between mortar joints or courses. Ties can also be bolted to existing walls to secure veneer.

Masonry Or Concrete Nails—Masonry nails are forged from case-hardened steel. They are used to join wood studs, furring strips and 2x4 plates to masonry walls and paving. They are available in several styles—round, square or fluted. Wear safety goggles and use a heavy ball-peen hammer for driving masonry nails. Never use a regular hammer!

Screw-In Anchors—These are all-purpose fasteners that can be used in hollow and solid walls and almost all materials. There are several different types. See chapter 5, page 156.

Expansion Bolt—Commonly called a *masonry bolt and anchor.* This bolt is used to fasten wood or metal materials to masonry joints or walls. See page 156.

Post Anchor Or Post Base—These fasteners anchor posts to concrete paving, wood decking or to poured-concrete walls. Many styles are available. Post anchors can be set into mortar joints of masonry walls. They are useful to elevate the post base. Use an expansion bolt to fasten post anchors to existing concrete. Use nails or bolts to attach post anchors to wood decks.

Special Anchors—Many different anchors are available or can be custom-made. They are set into wet concrete or mortar joints to hold benches to walls or other construction jobs. If special anchors are too expensive, experiment with other connectors.

Nails—There are many kinds of nails. Page 154 in chapter 5 has detailed information on all kinds of nails and their characteristics, sizes and uses.

Screws—These threaded fasteners provide more holding power than nails. Screws are more expensive and time-consuming to install. Holes must be predrilled for screws. Use screws for fastening hinges, latches and hardware. Screws are available in lengths by inches and diameter, style of head and type of metal. See page 154 in chapter 5.

Metal Connectors And Anchors—These fasteners are often used in combination with other fasteners. They provide more strength than nails, screws or bolts used alone.

REINFORCEMENT

Walls are strengthened or reinforced by several methods. Brick, concrete-block and poured-concrete walls use steel reinforcing bars, called *rebars* or *rods,* and masonry ties. Low walls are not always reinforced, but the use of rebar is a good idea in cold climates, or earthquake country. Local building codes usually require reinforcing for high walls.

Stone and rubble walls are reinforced by placing pieces of stone or rubble that span the width of the wall at regular intervals. These reinforcing pieces are called *bondstones.*

Brick walls are reinforced by the use of *headers.* See page 101. A header is a single brick turned to span the width of the wall. Headers tie two side-by-side tiers of bricks together. A *pilaster* is a special reinforcing column. See page 107.

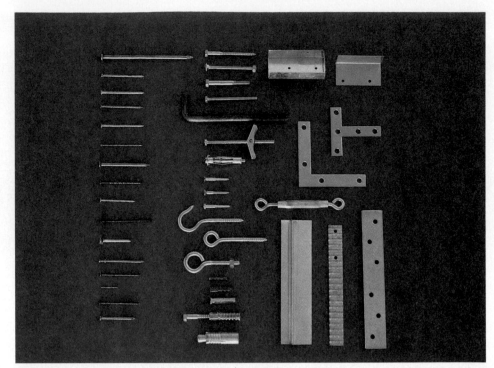

Selection Of Typical Fasteners. Left row: common spike, common nail, galvanized common nail, box nail, galvanized box nail, finish nail, masonry nail, cement-coated drive-screw nail, siding nail, annular ring nail, aluminum twist nail with neoprene washer, double-head duplex nail, cement-coated sinker nail, brad, vinyl-coated sinker nail, joist hanger nail. Center Row: lag bolt, carriage bolt and nut, machine bolt, stove bolt, J-shape anchor bolt, toggle bolt, molly bolt, flat-head screw, oval-head screw, round-head screw, screw hook, eye screw, eye bolt, fiber plug, plastic anchor, lead anchor. Right row: fence bracket, corner brace, T-plate, L-plate, turnbuckle, Z-bar, masonry tie, iron plate strap.

CAPPING THE WALL

Walls are capped to keep water from entering and give a finished appearance. This cap can be made from the same material as the wall or from a contrasting material. Common cap materials are poured concrete, bricks, tiles, concrete-block cap stones, flat stones and wood.

HARDWARE AND WIRING

Hardware, such as bolts for hinges or electrical wiring conduit, should be placed in mortar joints as walls are built.

Gate hardware placed in concrete block or hollow cavity walls requires the cavities be filled with concrete. The concrete secures the hardware and provides extra strength for gate supports.

Poured-concrete walls should have hardware or electrical fixtures in place during the pouring operation. Install lighting, doorbell and intercom systems during construction.

CONTROL JOINTS

Walls are subject to many stresses. These stresses produce cracks at predictable and unpredictable places. Cracks usually appear at changes in wall thickness or at pilasters and columns. Cracks occur at changes in wall height or where footings step down a slope.

Long walls may crack because supporting footings expand and contract at different rates than the wall. This expansion and contraction occurs during freezing and thawing cycles in cold climates. Cracks appear because footings settle over time. Earthquakes can also cause cracks.

To control these cracks, *control joints*—intentionally weakened vertical joints—are positioned as the wall is being built. Control joints are placed where cracks will *probably* appear. Control joints do not guarantee that other cracks will not occur. Cracks that do appear will form in a straight vertical line. This makes cracks less noticeable. Control joints should extend through stucco or veneer facing.

There are many methods for constructing control joints. Concrete blocks with control joints cast into them are available from suppliers.

Stucco wall with brick pilasters is capped by brick. Cap gives a neat, finished appearance and sheds water.

All hardware for electrical lights, intercom systems or gate hinges should be installed in masonry during the construction process.

Cracks that appear in concrete-block, brick or poured-concrete walls can be caused by inadequate footings, poor soil stability, earthquakes, frost heaving and poor-quality mortar or construction.

How To Build Walls   **83**

RETAINING WALLS

Retaining walls hold the weight of soil and must be constructed for extra strength.

Retaining walls and all walls higher than 3 feet usually must be designed by an engineer according to building codes and regulations. Check with local authorities. Requirements for retaining walls are for your safety. Low retaining walls, those under 3 feet high, may be designed and built by homeowners.

Retaining walls may be made of masonry materials and large timbers or railroad ties. See page 128 for construction details.

If a retaining wall is needed to hold a change of grade, it may be necessary to dig out soil and fill in the slope surfaces. This is commonly called *cutting and filling*. See the illustration below. Remove soil from behind the wall's position. Build the retaining wall and replace the soil behind the wall. Sprinkle soil with water and tamp down in 12-inch layers. This reduces further settling.

Low, concrete retaining walls hold soil and alter terrain. Plants growing over the wall soften harsh lines and add color.

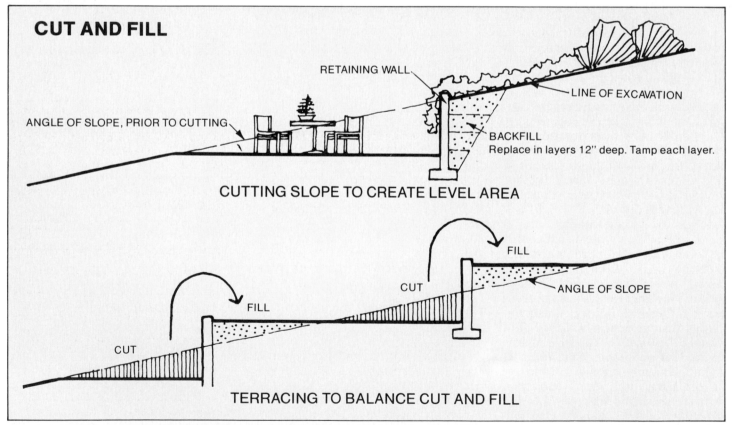

A cut-and-fill process is used to create level surfaces from sloping sites. The *cut* is the soil removed from the site. The *fill* is the soil placed on the site. Try to balance soil amounts from cutting and filling. To erect a retaining wall and make a level pad by cutting into a slope, dig out or cut the area behind the proposed wall. Build a footing and wall, then add backfill soil behind the wall. Place backfill soil in layers. Use excavated soil taken from slope. To terrace a slope and create level pads, dig out area of wall footing. Build footing and wall, then cut slope and add backfill soil behind the wall.

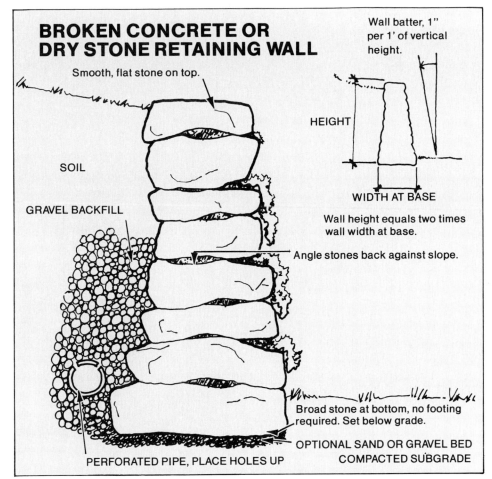

BROKEN CONCRETE OR DRY STONE RETAINING WALL

Smooth, flat stone on top.

SOIL

GRAVEL BACKFILL

Wall batter, 1" per 1' of vertical height.

HEIGHT

WIDTH AT BASE

Wall height equals two times wall width at base.

Angle stones back against slope.

Broad stone at bottom, no footing required. Set below grade.

OPTIONAL SAND OR GRAVEL BED
COMPACTED SUBGRADE

PERFORATED PIPE, PLACE HOLES UP

A dry wall made of stone or broken concrete is perfect for terracing slopes around trees. Plants inserted into gaps in stone joints soften the wall's appearance.

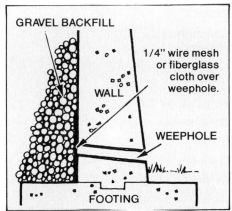

GRAVEL BACKFILL

1/4" wire mesh or fiberglass cloth over weephole.

WALL

WEEPHOLE

FOOTING

Drainage behind a retaining wall is essential. Weepholes are made by inserting plastic pipe into concrete formwork before wet concrete is poured. Weepholes can clog with soil. Use wire mesh or fiberglass cloth placed against the opening before backfilling soil.

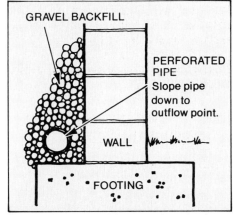

GRAVEL BACKFILL

PERFORATED PIPE
Slope pipe down to outflow point.

WALL

FOOTING

Drain pipe placed in gravel at the base of a retaining wall is the best way to carry away excess moisture. Perforated pipe is laid with holes up. Combine drain pipe with weepholes for extra water-carrying capacity. Pipe must slope down along the length of the wall to the outflow point.

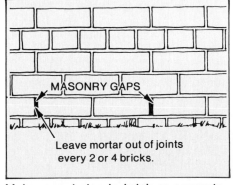

MASONRY GAPS

Leave mortar out of joints every 2 or 4 bricks.

Make weepholes in brick or concrete-block walls by omitting mortar from vertical joints as wall is built. Insert a wood dowel or stick between masonry units to keep weepholes from clogging with wet mortar. Place wire mesh or fiberglass cloth against back opening before backfilling soil.

Cutting and filling of earth can be done with a shovel and wheelbarrow. Bulldozers, backhoes or front-end loaders may be necessary for larger jobs. Heavy equipment may be rented, but only experienced operators should attempt to use it.

Preserve existing trees on any site. Digging and filling of soil around trees can cause injury to tree roots.

Drainage behind a retaining wall *must be* considered. Accumulation of water under or against a wall can cause the wall to collapse. Gravel or rock backfill used with weepholes or drainage tiles provides good drainage. See illustration at right.

Weepholes allow underground water to seep through a wall. Weepholes are easy to make. Make weepholes at the base of a wall by inserting plastic pipe or copper tubing at equally spaced intervals. Space weepholes approximately 2 feet apart. Make them 1 or 2 inches in diameter. Omitting an occasional mortar joint in the base course of masonry walls is an alternative way to provide weepholes. Weepholes will be the size of the joints, approximately 3/8 inch in width. It is a good idea to place this type of weephole every 2 or 4 bricks. See the illustration at right.

Drainage Tile is a special pipe with perforations or holes. It channels water away from the wall. Lay perforated drainage tile at the base of the wall under gravel backfill. Point the holes in the pipe *up*. Raise one end of the drain tile to create a slope so water can flow.

Parts of walls located below ground should be coated with asphalt or a layer of building paper to prevent moisture contact. Perforated building paper or fiberglass matting may be laid over gravel to prevent soil from filling in spaces. To grow plants next to walls, place 1 or 2 feet of soil on top of gravel. Gravel is not necessary in areas with fast-draining soils having little clay content.

How To Build Walls **85**

Concrete-block retaining wall holds soil on different levels. Weepholes allow for drainage.

CONCRETE-BLOCK RETAINING WALL

The following instructions are for building retaining walls and free-standing walls with concrete blocks. These walls should not be higher than 6 feet. Free-standing walls do not usually require steel reinforcing or draining provisions. The concrete-block retaining wall shown above is designed to blend into the hillside.

Footing—The footing for a concrete-block wall should be at least 12 inches wide and 12 inches deep. A deeper footing extending below the *frost line* may be needed in areas subject to frost heaving. The frost line is the lowest level in the soil that frost reaches.

Before digging the trench for a footing, lay out a dry course of concrete blocks to plan the footing. Base overall wall dimensions on block size.

Reinforcement—A concrete-block retaining wall must be reinforced with vertical, steel reinforcing rods. These rods are inserted in the concrete footing while it is still soft, at 2- to 4-foot intervals. Horizontal reinforcing rods or bond beams may also be required. Check local building codes for reinforcement requirements. See page 152 for more information.

Concrete Blocks

Concrete blocks are widely used as a strong building material. Blocks are made from cement, aggregate and water. Some concrete blocks are made with lightweight aggregates, such as pumice or cinder. Making blocks with lightweight aggregates gives higher fire resistance, and better acoustical and insulating properties. The weight of blocks is also reduced, making them easier to use.

Types Of Concrete Blocks—Most concrete blocks are made with three cores or hollow areas in each block. The end of each block is shaped to form a half core. When this half core is butted against another block with a half core, a small core is formed at the block joint.

Some blocks are made with tapered face shells and inner webs. The taper allows room for mortar when the blocks are laid and adds strength. Use tapered blocks with the wide or heavy side up.

Specific shaped concrete blocks have special uses.

Corner Blocks are flat on one end. Use corner blocks at the ends of walls.

Stretcher Blocks are flat on one face and have half cores at each end. Stretcher blocks are used between corners of walls.

Control-Joint Blocks have tongue-and-groove shaped ends. These blocks provide support to wall sections on each side of control joints.

Solid Blocks Or Cap Blocks can be solid or partially cored. Use solid blocks to cover interior cavities of walls.

Jamb Blocks have a cutout on one end and are used at the sides of wall openings. Jamb blocks are used where windows and doors will be placed.

Header Blocks have a cutout on one face side. Header blocks are used across the top and bottom of openings for windows or doors.

Size Of Blocks—Concrete blocks are nominally 8x8x16". This is the measurement of the block after a 3/8-inch mortar joint is applied. Eight-inch concrete blocks actually measure 7-5/8x7-5/8x15-5/8".

Most concrete blocks are 12 or 16 inches long. Blocks of these sizes have concave ends. Smaller 4- or 6-inch blocks have plain, flat ends.

Estimating Block Needs—Determining the number of blocks needed for a wall is easy. Measure the length of the proposed wall and multiply this number by the planned height. The resulting figure is the number of square feet in the wall. Divide the number of square feet by 100 to obtain the multiplication factor or multiplier. See the example below.

Length of wall: 75 feet
Height of wall: 4 feet
    75 x 4 = 300 square feet of wall surface area.
    300 ÷ 100 = 3 (Multiplier)
    3 x 112-1/2 = 337-1/2 blocks.

A standard 8x8x16" block requires 112-1/2 blocks per 100 square feet of surface area. Multiplying the number of blocks by the number of 100-square-foot sections equals 337-1/2 blocks needed. Add 5% to make sure you have enough blocks.

NUMBER OF BLOCKS REQUIRED FOR 100 SQUARE FEET OF WALL	
Block Size	Blocks per 100 sq. ft. of wall
4x4x16"	225
6x4x16"	225
8x4x16"	225
4x8x16"	112-1/2
6x8x16"	112-1/2
8x8x16" (Std. Size)	112-1/2
12x8x16"	112-1/2

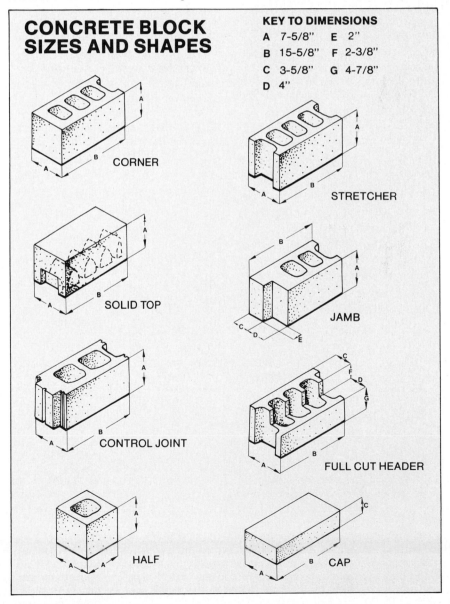

CONCRETE BLOCK SIZES AND SHAPES

KEY TO DIMENSIONS
A 7-5/8"   E 2"
B 15-5/8"   F 2-3/8"
C 3-5/8"   G 4-7/8"
D 4"

CORNER

STRETCHER

SOLID TOP

JAMB

CONTROL JOINT

FULL CUT HEADER

HALF

CAP

LAYING A BLOCK WALL

The first course of a block wall must be properly positioned to ensure the position of every block in the following courses.

The rest of the wall will be built on top of the first course. Adjustment in position cannot be made after the first course is set in mortar.

Practice Run—Make a dry run first. Place corner blocks in desired locations on the footing.

Place the remaining blocks, called *stretcher blocks,* between corner blocks. Allow an average of 3/8 inch between each block for mortar joints. Use a 3/8-inch-thick strip of wood as a spacing guide.

When all blocks are in the correct position, stretch a string guide line to mark the top outer edge of the first course. See instructions on page 78 for laying out and positioning *batter boards.* Batter boards are placed at corners to mark reference points.

Position the string approximately 1/4 inch away from the outer face of the wall to keep from touching it when laying blocks. Remove all blocks from the footing.

Laying The First Course—Spread a bed of mortar approximately 1 inch thick on the footing. The mortar bed should be long enough to set three blocks and as wide as the blocks. Make mortar bed edges thicker than the center of the bed.

Place corner blocks, with thick side up, into desired position. Use a *trowel,* a tool used for placing mortar, and tap corner block into mortar.

Be sure the corner block is aligned with the corner strings, horizontally level and vertically plumb. Use a carpenter's level to check plumb.

Place a stretcher block on end and spread a layer of mortar, approximately 3/4 inch thick, on the edges.

Place stretcher blocks in the mortar bed, with the mortared end against the corner block. Tap stretcher blocks in the mortar bed.

Repeat this process with the next two stretcher blocks. Make sure these blocks are aligned with the guide string and each other. Blocks must be horizontally level and vertically plumb. Mortar joints should not be wider than 3/8 inch. Remove excess mortar from joints.

After three blocks have been mortared in place, repeat the procedure at the other end of the wall. Remember to keep the mortar joints close to 3/8 inch thick. Mortar joints may vary slightly from 1/4 inch to 5/8 inch.

After three blocks at each end of the wall are mortared in place, place the remaining stretcher blocks.

It's important to make frequent checks to ensure blocks are aligned with the guide string and each other. Blocks must be horizontally level and vertically plumb.

Installing the last block in the first course can be difficult for beginners. Here is an easy method for installing this last block, called a *closure block.*

Spread a 3/4-inch-thick layer of mortar on both ends of the block. Spread a 3/4-inch layer of mortar on the ends of blocks on either side of the last block and on the course.

Carefully lower the last block, with mortared ends, into the opening. Tap it into position. Check that the block is even with the guide string and other blocks. Make sure it is horizontally level and vertically plumb. Remove any excess mortar from the joints.

Building Ends And Corners—Walls can end in one of three ways. They can join another wall, join at a corner

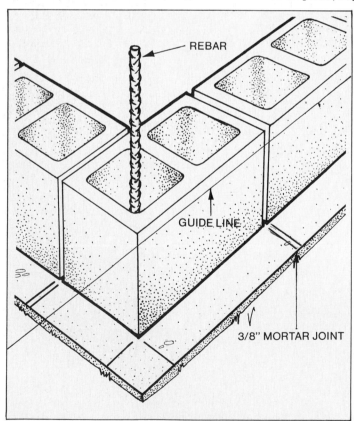

Mark the location of the wall's outer edge on footing. Lay dry course of blocks to determine block spacing. Allow 3/8-inch spacing for mortar joints. Mark spacing and ends of wall and set blocks aside. Do not wet concrete blocks.

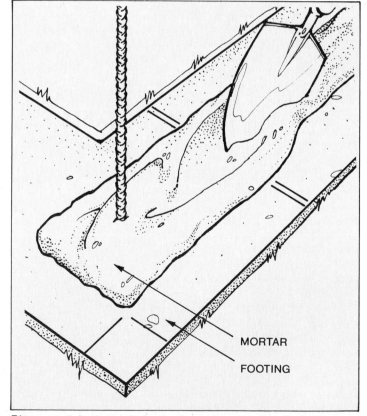

Place a 1-inch-thick bed of mortar on the footing. Lay enough mortar for three blocks. Furrow mortar in the center and distribute it to wall edges. Use a stiff mortar mix so it does not squeeze out under the weight of blocks.

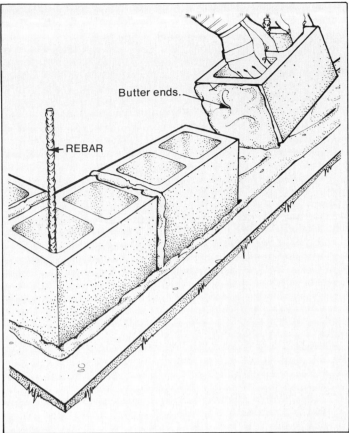

Butter ends.

← REBAR

After the mortar bed is laid, butter the end of all three blocks and set them on end. Lay corner block, then lay second and third blocks. Make 3/8-inch joints as you lay blocks in place. Make sure blocks are horizontally level and aligned with the string line. Tap blocks to force them level and in line. Lay base course three blocks at a time.

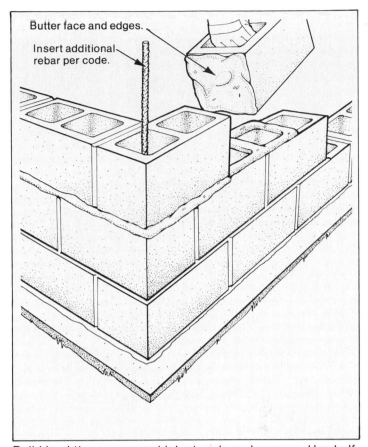

Butter face and edges.

Insert additional rebar per code.

Build lead three courses high at ends and corners. Use half blocks for even courses at ends. Turn blocks for corners. Mortar faces and edges of blocks at the same time bed joints are made. Use a storyboard to maintain horizontal joint thickness. Check for level and plumb on each surface. Build a second lead at other end or corner.

or end as a straight edge.

Ends are built up after the first course is mortared in place. The end of a free-standing wall should be built up several courses ahead of stretcher courses.

Use a *storyboard* to ensure that the top of one end is the same height as the other end. A storyboard is a tall board marked in 4- and 8-inch increments. It is placed next to a wall to measure the height of each course of bricks or blocks. See page 100.

Make constant checks to ensure the faces of all blocks are even with each other. The ends of all blocks must also be even. Keep each end course level and plumb.

Corner courses should also be built up several courses ahead of stretcher courses. Use a storyboard to check the height of each corner. Both corners must be the same height.

Use half blocks or full-size corner blocks lengthwise in alternate courses of each wall. This ensures that vertical mortar joints are staggered.

Mason's level is used to check masonry courses for level, to check wall faces for vertical or horizontal bulge, and to check wall ends and corners for plumb.

Building Stretcher Courses—After the first course is laid and corners or ends are started, stretcher courses can be mortared in place.

Remember to place reinforcing bars or masonry ties where required. The position of control joints should be marked too.

Stretch a string between built-up corners or ends to mark the position of the top edge of the next course. This string will be level if the first corner and end courses are level. Check level with a line level and adjust as necessary.

Spread mortar on the face edges of blocks in the bottom course. Local building codes may require a full mortar bed. If a full mortar bed is required, spread mortar on cross webs of the block. This mortar bed should be approximately 3/4 inch thick. Spread a 3/4-inch layer of mortar on the ends of blocks to be positioned.

Place blocks in the mortar bed with the mortared end against the previous block in the course. Tap the block into the mortar bed.

Make sure vertical and horizontal mortar joints are approximately 3/8 inch thick. Again, check that all blocks are aligned with the guide string and each other, and that blocks are horizontally level and vertically plumb. This is an important procedure and should be repeated every three or four blocks.

Set the last block in each course the same way as the last block in the first course. Remove excess mortar from all joints before it dries and hardens.

Tool joints as required. See page 103 for ways to tool mortar joints.

Repeat the laying procedure for each course of blocks. When the next to last course is mortared in place, the wall is ready to be capped.

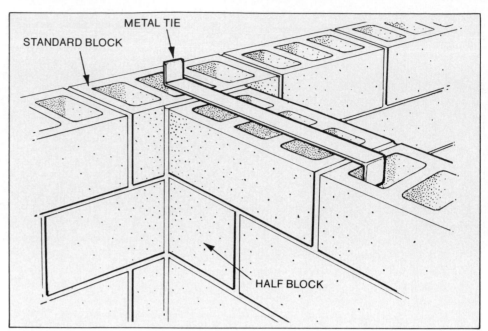

Metal masonry ties are used to tie two wall sections together. The tie shown here is used to tie walls at a 90° angle to each other. The same tie could be used at corners for added reinforcement.

Continue to add blocks between leads. Keep a careful check on 3/8-inch spacing between mortar joints. Add horizontal reinforcing as specified by local building codes. Cut closure block to size and lower in place with mortar on all edges of opening and block ends. Stagger closure block positions in each course so they do not align with each other.

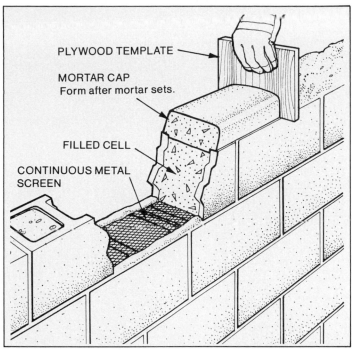

PLYWOOD TEMPLATE

MORTAR CAP
Form after mortar sets.

FILLED CELL

CONTINUOUS METAL
SCREEN

Before laying the top course, cover the next-to-last course of blocks with wire mesh or building paper. To finish the top of a wall, fill the top course of blocks with mortar. All cells containing reinforcing bars should be filled with mortar. Screed off excess mortar. Form a mortar cap by using a plywood template to shape stiff mortar.

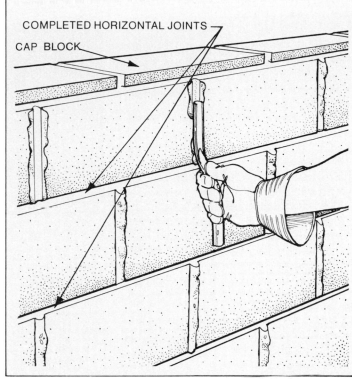

COMPLETED HORIZONTAL JOINTS

CAP BLOCK

After mortar has set, but is still workable, strike mortar joints. Tool horizontal joints first, then vertical joints. Concave or V-shaped joints are traditional. Other styles give surface texture variety. See page 103.

Capping The Wall—Concrete block walls can be capped in several ways. One way is to fill the top course with mortar and strike it smooth. Form a rounded concrete cap with a curved template and stiff concrete mix.

Cover the next to last course of blocks with steel mesh or building paper before laying and filling the top course with *grout* or mortar. Grout is a thinned-mortar mix made by adding more water to mortar. The mesh keeps concrete from falling to the bottom of the wall.

Concrete cap blocks or clay brick may be used to cap a wall. Redwood or cedar boards, 2 inches thick, can also be used. Use anchor bolts set in grouted cells to attach wood caps.

Wall Finishes—Concrete block walls accept a variety of finishes. Stone veneer may be attached to walls with mortar. See page 92. Brick facing may be applied using mortar and metal ties. Stucco finishes can create an interesting surface texture. See stucco walls on page 126.

Masonry or latex paints are durable finishes. Wait until mortar joints have dried before painting the wall. Masonry paint must be scrubbed into damp blocks with a wire brush. Latex paint is applied with a long-napped roller.

Wall adjacent to entryway is capped with used brick, effectively complementing the used-brick walk.

Veneer Facings For Walls

Thin rock or stone facings are used to change the appearance of new or old masonry walls. These facings are called *veneers*. The most popular use of veneers is as a covering for concrete-block walls. Veneers make concrete-block walls look the same as stone or brick. The cost, depending on various factors, may be less than half the cost for solid brick or natural stone walls.

There are many different types of veneers available. Veneers are made from thin pieces of natural or synthetic stone, cement, thin brick and whole stone or brick. Corner pieces are available for many styles of veneers. Choose veneers that improve the appearance of the wall.

Align weepholes in veneer coverings with retaining-wall weepholes and control joints.

APPLYING THIN-FACE VENEER ON UNPAINTED MASONRY

Apply a thin layer of mortar to a clean wall surface. Place veneer in the desired pattern, alternating corner pieces. Fit veneer together for a tight, unmortared appearance. After veneer is attached, fill joints with mortar using a grout bag. Finish or tool joints as desired.

APPLYING THIN-FACE VENEER ON PAINTED OR IRREGULAR SURFACES

Attach 1-inch-mesh chicken wire or self-furring wire lath to the wall surface with masonry nails. Spread a coat of mortar over the wire and score it with a stiff wire brush. This mortar is called the *scratch coat.* Allow the scratch coat to cure. Apply a second coat of mortar and place veneer in desired pattern. Finish the job by jointing.

APPLYING WHOLE-STONE OR BRICK VENEER

New Walls—*Masonry ties* are needed to attach bricks or stone veneer to walls. Masonry ties are small strips of metal that "tie" both the wall and veneer together. Attach masonry ties in new walls by inserting them in mortar joints between courses as the wall is being built. Space ties approximately 16 inches apart vertically and 32 inches apart horizontally.

The wall of this fence-and-veneered-wall combination follows ground slope. Natural stone veneer blends with landscape. The top of the wall and fence remain level. Post anchors were inserted in mortar joints between stones.

Existing Walls—Attach ties to an existing wall using screw-in fiber plugs. Drill holes in mortar joints and install the plugs. Screw masonry ties in the holes. Space ties the same as for new walls. Offset rows of ties so they do not line up vertically. Apply mortar to the existing wall and set veneer in position. The ties are the anchors that hold the two surfaces together.

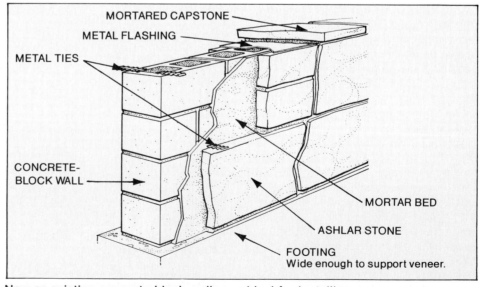

New or existing concrete-block walls are ideal for installing veneer masonry surfaces. This example shows how ashlar stone is attached to an existing concrete-block wall. An initial coat of mortar is spread on the block wall, then ashlar stone is mortared in place over mortar coat. Note use of metal ties to bond stone to block wall. Flashing is placed on top course to prevent moisture from entering the wall.

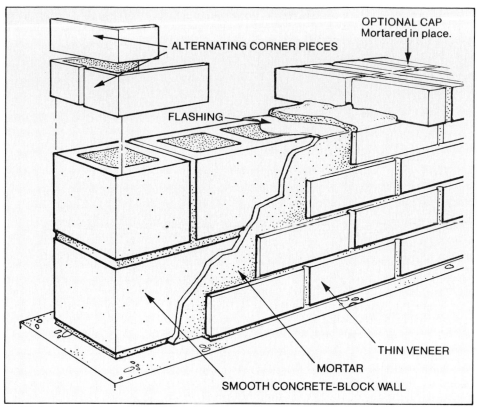

Artificial or real brick veneer can be attached over smooth concrete-block walls. Mortar is spread on the block wall, then veneer is set in place. After mortar has set, bricks are grouted and jointed.

Artificial brick-veneer corner piece is placed over corners of concrete-block or poured-concrete walls.

Artificial brick-veneer siding. Natural brick veneer and corner pieces are also available. Whole brick may also be used as a veneer.

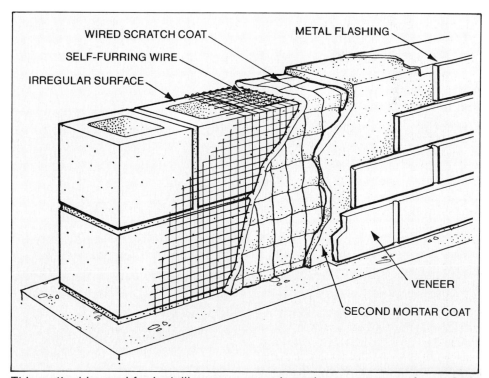

This method is used for installing veneer over irregular or uneven surfaces. Self-furring wire is attached to the existing wall with masonry nails. A scratch coat of mortar and wire is applied over the wire and allowed to dry. A second, thicker coat of mortar is applied and veneer is set in place. After the mortar has set, all joints are grouted and struck.

How To Build Walls 93

Brick Walls

Brick walls have been used for hundreds of years and are always in style. As a building material, brick is permanent, has natural beauty and is easy to use. Brick walls are attractive in any garden, bringing warmth and texture into the landscape.

The small size of the bricks makes them easy to work with. Wall construction usually takes some time. Don't be in a hurry in designing or building a brick wall. Take time to plan the style and location. Follow the step-by-step instructions provided here and the result will be a well-built wall that will last for years.

Brick-wall styles range from low seating walls to tall garden walls, solid retaining walls or open screening walls. There is a style for nearly every garden need.

This mixture of veneers is a display wall. It was built to show a few of the brick-veneer products available.

Attractive brick wall with pilasters has shadowline formed by extruded brick course.

Brick types, sizes and bond patterns must be considered in designing walls.

Structural elements, such as footings and reinforcement, must also be considered. The thickness, height and amount of reinforcing for various brick walls are interrelated. Check local building codes for legal restrictions and building specifications for height, width, reinforcement requirements and property locations before building a wall.

Footings—All brick garden walls should have a concrete footing. Make the footing twice the width of the wall and extend the footing below the frost line. See footings, page 74.

Reinforcement—Brick walls can be reinforced with structural bonds called *header courses*. This is known as *masonry reinforcement*. In double-wythe walls, the header course ties the wall faces together. A *wythe* is a term used to describe the width of one course, usually one brick or 4 inches. A double-wythe wall is 8 inches wide, or two bricks thick.

Common, English, Flemish and Rowlock brick bonds all use header courses. See page 104 for descriptions of these brick laying patterns.

Another type of masonry reinforcement is the *pilaster*. Pilasters are placed in tall garden walls at 12-foot intervals. Pilasters are tied into the wall with overlapping bricks in alternate courses.

Steel masonry ties are placed between brick courses when building walls. They span two wythes, tying them together. Masonry ties are 3/16 inch in diameter and come in a Z or rectangular shape. See illustration below left.

Masonry ties should be placed across two wythes every 36 inches along a course. The ties should be placed at least 18 inches apart vertically. Stagger the placement of ties so they are not directly above each other.

The cavity in the center of the wall can be grouted. It can also be reduced to the width of a mortar joint. This results in a slightly narrower wall.

Types Of Brick—Bricks are made from clay and baked in large ovens or *kilns* until hard. Most brick is of the

REINFORCING BRICK MASONRY

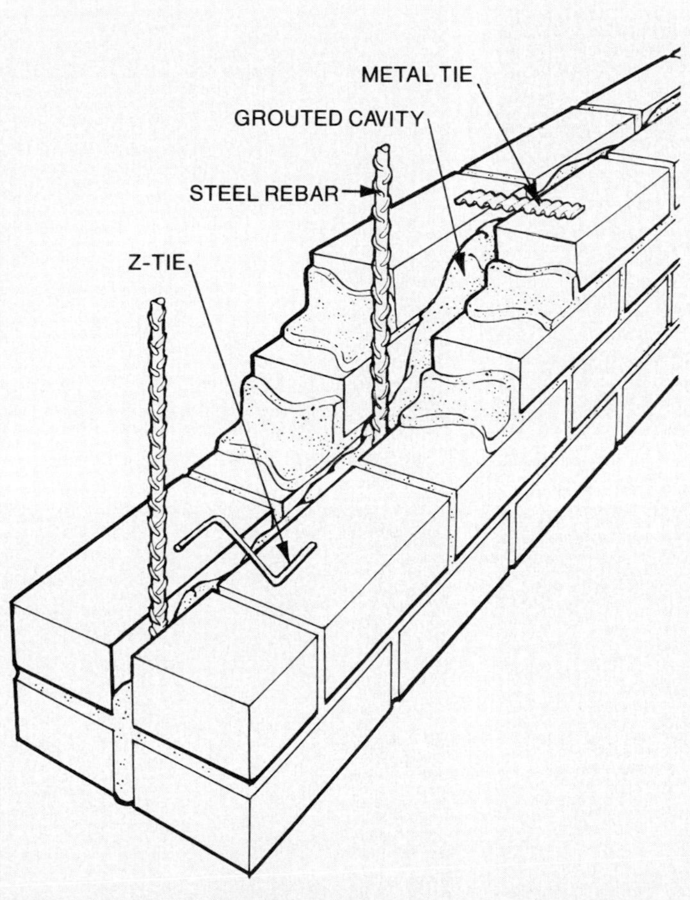

METAL TIE

GROUTED CAVITY

STEEL REBAR

Z-TIE

Reinforcing tall running-bond or stack-bond walls and retaining walls is essential to give structural strength. Reinforcing specifications vary with local codes. Bond patterns with headers may not need steel reinforcing. Walls less than 2 feet in height do not need reinforcing. Rebar is inserted in a footing when poured. Additional rebar is wired in to extend footing rebar. Cavities are filled with grout. Grout must surround rebar to make a solid structure. Use steel masonry ties laid in mortar joints to tie two wythes together with no bonding headers.

ADOBE BRICKS

Adobe is a traditional construction material used for hundreds of years in the American Southwest. A wall of adobe bricks complements early Spanish and native-American architecture. Its natural-earth color adds warmth to the landscape.

Traditional adobe bricks are made by mixing moist clay with straw and forming the mixture into bricks or blocks. The bricks are dried in the sun or fired in a kiln. Traditional adobe bricks eventually disintegrate when exposed to the weather. Modern adobe bricks are made with an asphalt-based stabilizer to make them more weather resistant. Walls made with untreated bricks can be covered with stucco or treated with a water sealer, such as *Thompsons Water Seal*, or a commercial masonry sealer.

Sizes—Adobe bricks for walls are generally much larger than ordinary clay bricks. They are commonly 16 inches long and 4 inches thick. Widths range from 3-1/2 to 12 inches. Larger adobe bricks are heavy—they can weigh up to 45 pounds. This makes them difficult to work with on walls over 4 feet tall.

How To Lay—The method for laying adobe bricks is similar to that for clay bricks, described on this page.

Because adobe bricks are heavy, they require a stable foundation. A strong concrete footing should extend below the frost line so the wall won't be affected by shifting soil.

Adobe walls higher than 2 feet should be reinforced with 1/4-inch reinforcing rods. Check local codes for footing and reinforcement requirements. One-wythe walls higher than 30 inches should be strengthened with pilasters spaced a maximum of 12 feet apart. Use the same mortar mix used for laying concrete blocks and bricks. See page 151 for mixing instructions.

common or building-brick variety and is used for basic wall construction. Different colors and textures are available.

Size Of Brick—All brick dimensions are nominal. The dimensions include the thickness of the mortar joint. *Common bricks* are 4 inches wide, 8 inches long and 2-2/3 inches high. Three courses or tiers of common bricks, with mortar between them, will build to a height of 8 inches.

Norman bricks are 4 inches wide, 12 inches long and 2-2/3 inches high. *Economy bricks* are 4 inches wide, 8 inches long and 4 inches high. *Roman bricks* are 4 inches wide, 12 inches long and 2 inches high.

Estimating Brick Quantities— The number of bricks needed for a wall can be estimated by using the table at right. Add 5% for wastage.

The table shows the approximate number of bricks for 100 square feet of wall, when bricks are laid in a normal wythe pattern and positioned as stretchers.

To figure the square footage of a wall, multiply the length of the wall by the height. This will give you the number of square feet in the wall. Divide this number by 100 and you'll have the number of 100-square-foot sections in the wall. Walls two or three wythes wide require double or triple quantities.

NUMBER OF BRICKS NEEDED FOR 100 SQUARE FEET OF WALL Use for single-wythe walls in running bond	
Brick size	**Number of bricks per 100 sq. ft.**
4x2-3/8x8"	675
4x3-1/5x8"	563
4x4x8"	450
4x5-1/3x8"	338
4x2x12"	600
4x2-2/3x12"	450
4x3-1/5x12"	375
4x4x12"	300
4x5-1/3x12"	225
6x2-2/3x12"	450
6x3-1/5x12"	375
6x4x12"	300

Traditional red brick, standard size.

Simulated used-brick is cheaper and more available than real used brick.

Fawn-colored, standard-size brick.

Concrete brick is available in gray and other colors and several different textures.

Buff-colored fire bricks withstand heat.

Simulated clinker-brick imitates old-fashioned clinkers. Clinkers are extremely hard.

Laying Bricks—After footings have been poured and allowed to cure, the next step is to lay the brick wall. Begin by making a trial or dry run without mortar. Determine the exact locations of corner bricks at each end of the wall. Use batter boards and string to mark this location. See page 78 to construct batter boards.

Stretch a string guide line to mark the top outer edge of the first brick course. Locate the line about 1/4 inch away from the face of the wall. This placement avoids hitting the string as bricks are laid.

Place the first course of bricks between the corner or end bricks. Use a 3/8-inch-thick board as a spacing guide between bricks. Remember to take into account the design and pattern of the wall. See page 104 for photographs of common patterns.

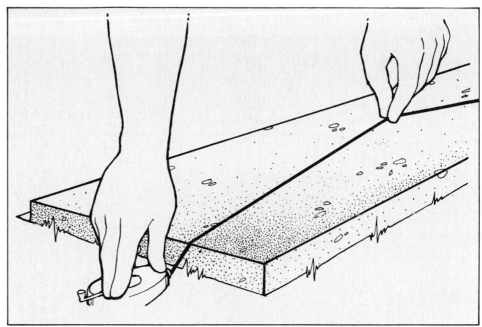

Locate outer edge of wall on footing. Snap a chalkline to mark wall outline. Use 3-4-5 triangle layout method described on page 78 to position corners or ends.

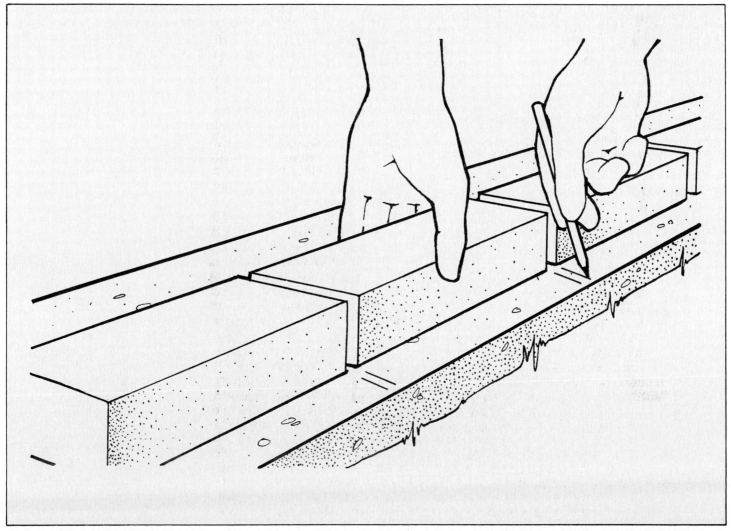

After marking wall location, lay a dry course along chalkline. Allow 1/2-inch space between bricks for mortar. Mark space on footing, then remove bricks.

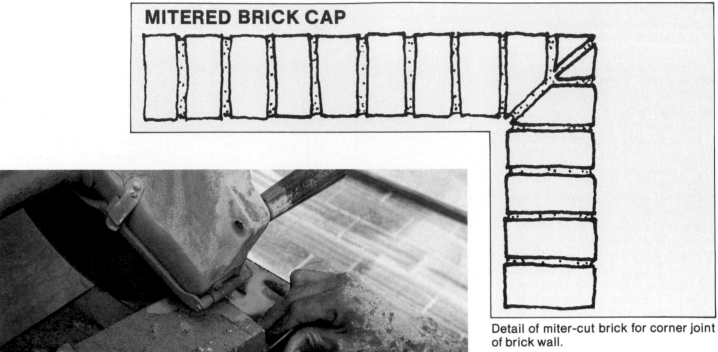

MITERED BRICK CAP

Brick water saw precisely and easily cuts bricks. It is especially useful for detailed mitering or where designs call for multiple closures.

Detail of miter-cut brick for corner joint of brick wall.

When laying out the dry run, it may be necessary to cut some bricks. Bricks can be cut using a *brickset* or mason's chisel and hammer.

To cut a brick, mark and score the brick on both sides. Put the brick on a smooth bed of wet sand. Place the brickset in the score mark and hit it with a hammer. The brick should break along the score line. See the photographs below.

To cut brick, mark cut-line by tapping with brickset. Score brick completely around while brick rests on sand or soil.

Position brickset on score line and strike brickset with mason's hammer or mallet. Electric power saw with special masonry blade may also be used to cut brick.

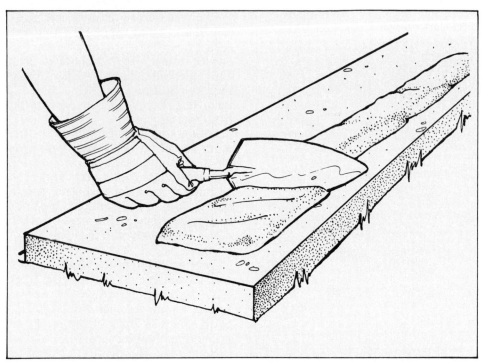

After you are satisfied with the position and spacing of bricks in the dry run, remove them from the footing. Spread a bed of mortar on the footing. The mortar bed should be as wide as the wall is thick and long enough to place three bricks. The mortar should be approximately 1 inch thick on the footing.

Make the edges of the mortar bed thicker than the center of the bed.

Lay the first corner brick into the correct position on the mortar bed. Spread a layer of mortar on the side or end of the next brick. Lay this brick in the mortar bed next to the first corner brick. Repeat this procedure until several bricks have been laid in the mortar.

Mix and place bed of mortar on footing three bricks long. Make the bed about 1 inch thick. Make a furrow in the mortar bed so mortar is almost as wide as the brick. Press first corner brick in place until mortar squeezes out to the edges. Bed joint should be about 1/2 inch thick when finished. Bricks should be damp before laying or they can absorb moisture from the mortar, reducing bond strength. Moisten brick pile 15 minutes before work starts.

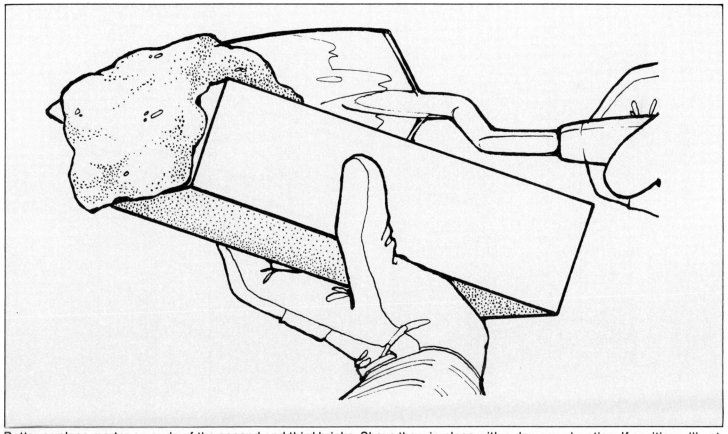

Butter or place mortar on ends of the second and third bricks. Shove them in place with a downward motion. If cavities will not be filled with mortar or grout, make weepholes in the base course. Space weepholes every two or four bricks by omitting mortar. Hold joint open with a wood dowel or pencil.

How To Build Walls 99

BACKUP COURSE

BASE COURSE

Complete base course working three bricks at a time. Check level as you work, tapping bricks into bed with trowel handle. Check joints for proper thickness. Trim off excess mortar with trowel and reuse it. Lay backup course three bricks at a time in the same manner as the first course. Match height of first wythe, using a header brick across the wall. Then check width. Don't mortar between the two wythes except at ends of wall.

Check to make sure bricks are properly aligned with the guide string and each other. Use a carpenter's level to ensure bricks are horizontally level and vertically plumb. Check that mortar joints are about 3/8 inch to 1/2 inch wide. Remove any excess mortar from mortar joints.

Follow the same procedure for the other end of the wall. After both ends of a wall are laid, the remaining stretcher bricks in the first course can be laid. Work from each end toward the middle. Apply mortar to brick ends and place them next to each other. Constantly check alignment of bricks as they are laid.

The last brick in the first course is the *closure brick*. The closure brick must be positioned carefully. Spread mortar about 3/4 inch thick on each of the sides or ends of the bricks on either side of the closure.

Spread a 3/4-inch-thick layer of mortar on the ends of the closure brick. Carefully slide the closure brick into position without knocking mortar out of the joints. Align the closure brick.

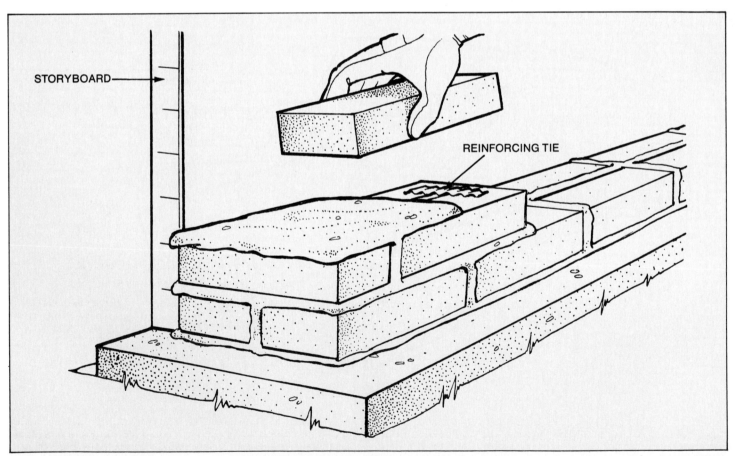

STORYBOARD

REINFORCING TIE

Build a lead five courses high at ends and corners. Turn every other end brick as a header to span wall to create running-bond pattern. Use a storyboard to maintain correct horizontal joint spacing. Join the two wythes with reinforcing ties.

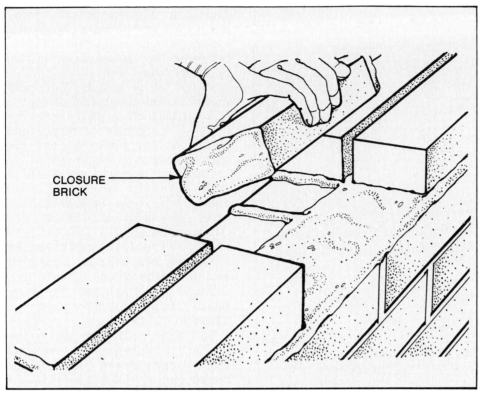

CLOSURE BRICK

Closure bricks are necessary to fill the wall length of each course. Allow 1/2 inch space for mortar and cut closure bricks to fill space. Butter both ends of closure brick and lay it straight down. Remove excess mortar squeezed from joint. Stagger position of closure bricks so they do not align vertically with adjacent courses. Build the backup course, checking for accuracy in height and level. Use storyboard, string and level. Continue building wall in five-course leads. Check constantly for accuracy.

After laying the first course, the corner or ends of the wall are built up. The corners or ends are built several courses ahead of the stretcher courses. Alternate and stagger corner bricks as shown on page 105.

When corners have been built up, lay the remaining stretcher courses in the same way as the first course.

Different laying patterns or thicknesses in bricks will determine the position of the bricks. See the illustrations on page 104 for these patterns.

The final layer of bricks placed on top of a wall is called the *header course*. The bricks are usually laid with the ends facing out and the length across the wall. See illustration, page 102.

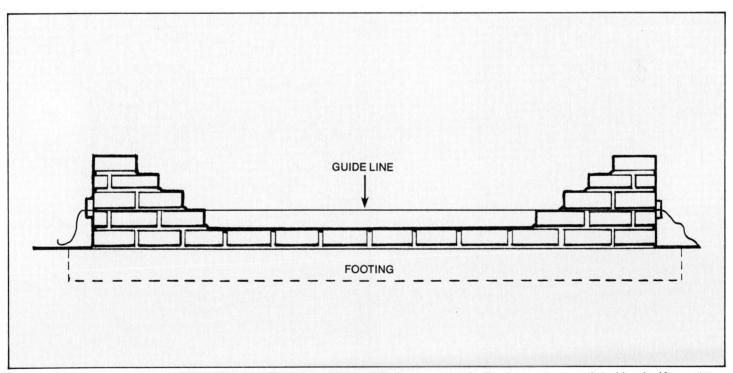

GUIDE LINE

FOOTING

Build leads at opposite ends of base course. Stretch a string guide line or mason's line between completed leads. Keep string 1/4 inch away from wall and flush with upper edge of course. Line can sag if wall is long. Periodically check height with storyboard. Lay brick courses from ends toward middle. Use line to maintain level. Move line up for succeeding courses. Check wall face for plumb as you work.

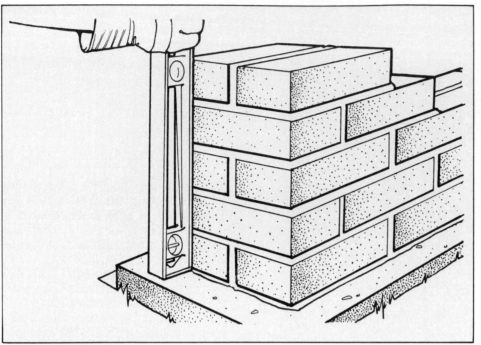

Continue to build up the end or corner of wall. Check for plumb and level on each surface as you build. Use a mason's level, string line and storyboard. Wall face must not bulge and courses must be level.

x

Finishing Mortar Joints—Mortar joints must be finished or tooled after the mortar stiffens, but before it becomes too hard. Joints can be finished in several ways.

Mortar can be troweled flush with the bricks. This is called a *flush joint*.

A special tool, called a *jointer*, can be used to compact the mortar into the joints. The jointer smooths the mortar joint into a concave shape.

The point of a trowel can be used to *strike* the mortar joint. Struck joints give an even look because the top edges of the bricks are carefully leveled and aligned.

A trowel can also be used to *weather* the mortar joint. Weather joints have an uneven appearance.

Mortar joints can also be *raked*. Raked mortar joints have mortar removed to a specific depth.

Tuck-point joints have the mortar removed the same as raked joints, but grout is then spread back into the mortar joint.

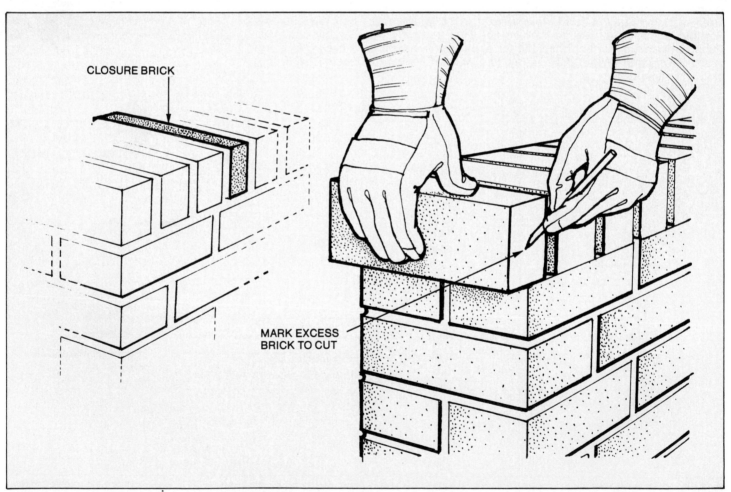

Wall cavity can be filled with grout and flashing added before capping wall. Flashing is recommended. A rowlock cap of header bricks unites the wythes and is the simplest cap. First, lay cap dry. Leave 1/2-inch joints to measure for a closure brick. Mark amount of excess brick to be cut. Cut closure brick and position it four bricks from end.

TYPES OF MORTAR JOINTS

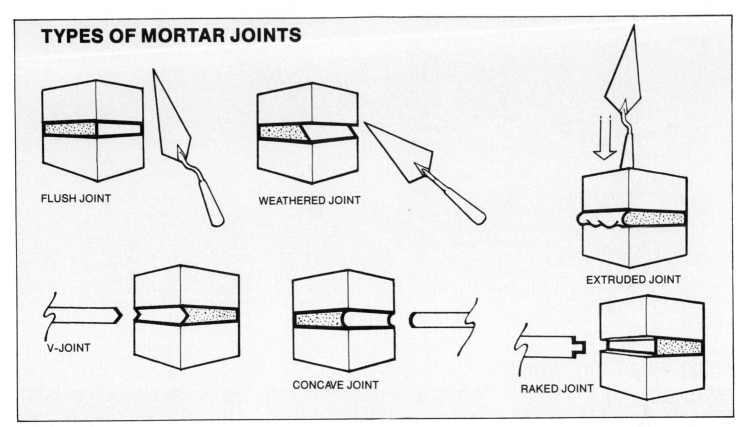

FLUSH JOINT

WEATHERED JOINT

EXTRUDED JOINT

V-JOINT

CONCAVE JOINT

RAKED JOINT

Types Of Mortar Joints

Flush Joint—Produces a smooth surface. Popular for walls that have a painted, whitewashed or stuccoed finish. This joint is not weathertight without finish. Formed with a wood float or trowel edge.

Weathered Joint—Watertight joint that allows moisture to drain off. Popular for brick work. Makes a nice shadow line. Formed with trowel.

Concave Joint—Excellent watertight joint because moisture drains off. Popular for concrete-block and brick walls. Gives walls a flat look. Formed with a special jointing tool, 1/2-inch bar, dowel or fingers.

Extruded Joint—This joint is not watertight. Painting improves water seal. A rustic-looking joint that gives texture to the wall surface. Joint is formed as bricks or blocks are laid. Bricks are tapped in place, forcing mortar out of joints.

V-Joint—Excellent watertight joint because moisture drains off. Popular for concrete-block and brick walls. Emphasizes shadows on wall surface. Formed with special jointing tool or corner of 1/2-inch square bar.

Raked Joint—Joints collect water and are not weathertight. Popular for brick and always used for stone masonry. Produces attractive shadow lines on wall surface. Downplays importance of mortar in design, providing rich appearance. Use special tool or dull-pointed stick. Rake joints 1/2 inch back for brick, 1/2 to 3/4 inch back for stone.

Strike joints with a jointing tool before mortar hardens. Strike horizontal or bed joints first, then strike vertical or head joints.

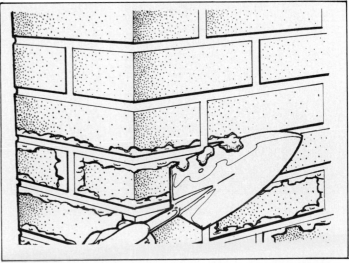

Remove excess mortar or *tags* with trowel. *Tags* are excess mortar forced out of joints. Then restrike vertical joints for a clean appearance.

After mortar has dried, use a wire brush to remove gritty residue from wall surface.

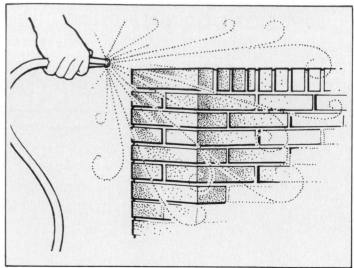

Keep wall moist for at least four days, allowing the mortar to cure slowly. Use a fine spray of water to wet wall.

BRICK-WALL PATTERNS

Running Bond

Common Bond

English Bond

Stack Bond or Jack-On-Jack

Rowlock Bond

Flemish Bond

LAYING BRICK-WALL PATTERNS

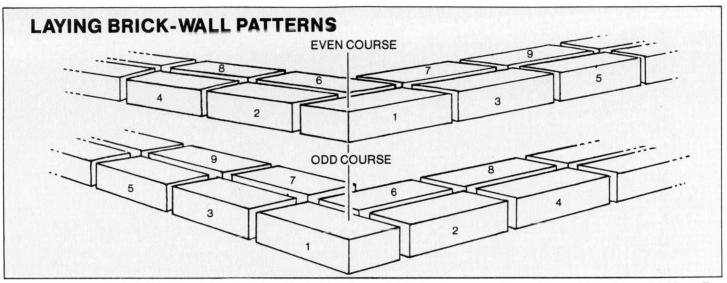

EVEN COURSE

ODD COURSE

The numbers on the bricks above indicate the order that bricks are laid in each course. The *odd* course is always laid first. The second course is even, the third odd, and so forth.

Below are a few of the many attractive ways to lay brick-wall patterns. Some of these designs require a great deal of closure cutting. Bricks are laid in odd and even courses. The numbers on bricks indicate the order bricks are laid in each course.

JACK-ON-JACK OR STACK BOND

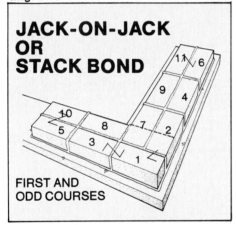

FIRST AND ODD COURSES

First And Odd Courses—This pattern can be built around rebar extending up from footing. Reinforcing ties and headers bond the two wythes together. Lay first and odd courses in order shown. Lay backup wythe last. Brick indicated by dotted line is for wall with no corner.

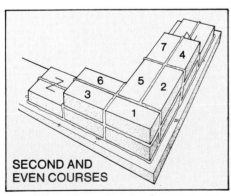

SECOND AND EVEN COURSES

Second And Even Courses—Lay second and even courses in order shown. Lay backup wythe last. Use masonry ties. Cavity can be filled with grout.

COMMON BOND

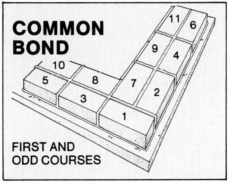

FIRST AND ODD COURSES

First And Odd Courses—This bond pattern makes reinforcing bars and ties unnecessary. Headers tie wythes together. Common-bond pattern is excellent for low walls. Lay first and odd courses in order shown.

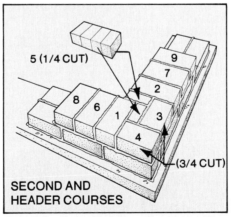

5 (1/4 CUT)

(3/4 CUT)

SECOND AND HEADER COURSES

Second And Header Courses—The second course is all headers. Lay headers in order shown. Cut 3/4-size closures and 1/4-size closures to fill in corner. Lay following courses in running bond, illustrated page 106. Repeat header course construction method every fifth or sixth course, then repeat running-bond pattern.

FLEMISH BOND

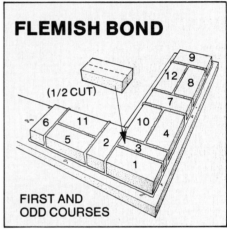

(1/2 CUT)

FIRST AND ODD COURSES

First And Odd Courses—This pattern uses alternating headers and stretchers in each course. Stretchers are centered over headers and overlap bottom stretcher by 1/4. Lay first and odd courses in order shown. Cut 1/2-size closures for corners.

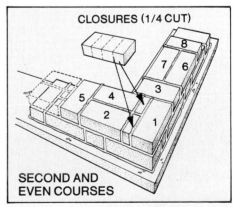

CLOSURES (1/4 CUT)

SECOND AND EVEN COURSES

Second And Even Courses—Lay second and even courses in order shown. Cut 1/4-size closures for corners. Dotted lines illustrate method for ending wall.

ENGLISH BOND

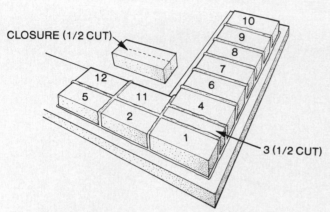

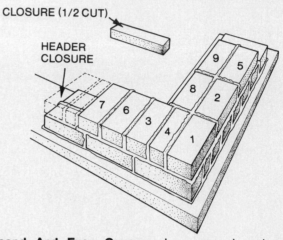

First And Odd Courses—This traditional pattern uses alternating courses of headers and stretchers. On one wall face, the header course is the first course. On the other wall face the header course is the second course. Lay first and odd courses in order shown. Cut 1/2-size closure and place it at the corner.

Second And Even Courses—Lay second and even course in order shown. Use 1/2-size closure and place it at the corner. Closure and header, shown with dotted lines, illustrate method for ending wall.

RUNNING BOND

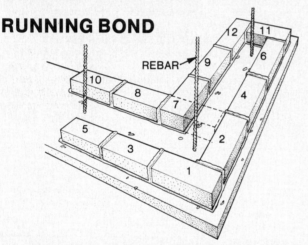

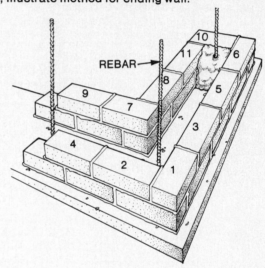

First And Odd Courses—To create a wider wall in the running-bond pattern, make a wider cavity using stretchers, shown with dotted lines. Stretchers are placed between the two wythes and wall ends. Check local codes for reinforcement requirements. Lay first and odd courses in order shown.

Second And Even Courses—Lay second and even courses in order shown. Use a stretcher to close cavity end. Fill cavity with grout if reinforcing is used. Cap the wall.

ROWLOCK BOND

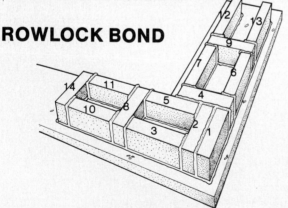

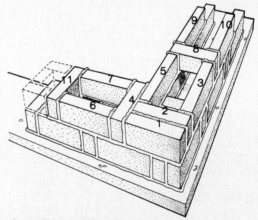

First And Odd Courses—Alternating headers and stretchers laid on edge create a wide cavity. This can be filled with grout and reinforced with rebars as local code specifies. This economical pattern makes a low seat wall or tall garden bond. Lay first and odd courses in order shown.

Second And Even Courses—Lay second and even courses in order shown. Use closures, shown with dotted lines, to end wall pattern. Cap the wall.

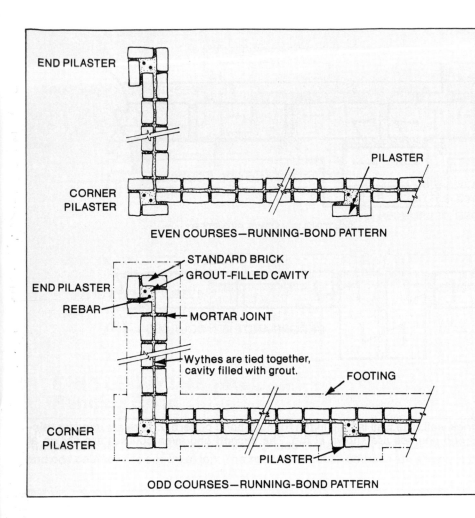

END PILASTER

CORNER PILASTER

PILASTER

EVEN COURSES—RUNNING-BOND PATTERN

STANDARD BRICK

GROUT-FILLED CAVITY

END PILASTER

REBAR

MORTAR JOINT

Wythes are tied together, cavity filled with grout.

FOOTING

CORNER PILASTER

PILASTER

ODD COURSES—RUNNING-BOND PATTERN

Pilasters For Walls

Brick and concrete-block walls often require pilasters for additional support and reinforcement. Pilasters may be built in the middle or at ends and corners of walls. Pilasters may extend on both sides of a wall, on one side or on alternating sides. The illustrations in this section show several different alternatives for brick and concrete-block walls.

Layout of first and odd courses for wall in running-bond pattern is shown in top view. Pilasters are located at corners, end of wall and middle of wall. Place pilasters no more than 12 feet apart. Here, pilasters are spaced 6 full bricks apart. Layout of second and even courses is shown in bottom illustration.

SECTION THROUGH WALL

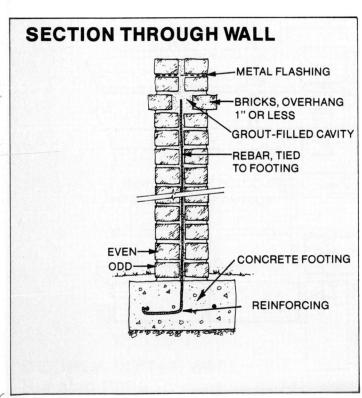

METAL FLASHING

BRICKS, OVERHANG 1" OR LESS

GROUT-FILLED CAVITY

REBAR, TIED TO FOOTING

EVEN

ODD

CONCRETE FOOTING

REINFORCING

An enlarged detail section of the wall shows construction techniques and materials.

CAPITAL CONSTRUCTION DETAIL

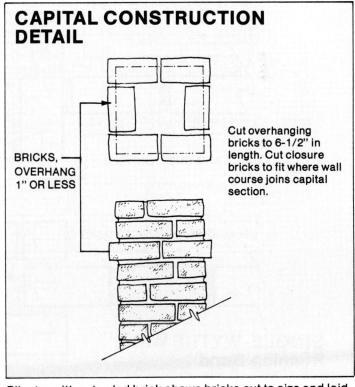

BRICKS, OVERHANG 1" OR LESS

Cut overhanging bricks to 6-1/2" in length. Cut closure bricks to fit where wall course joins capital section.

Pilaster with extruded brick shows bricks cut to size and laid over pilaster. Cut bricks are shown by dotted lines.

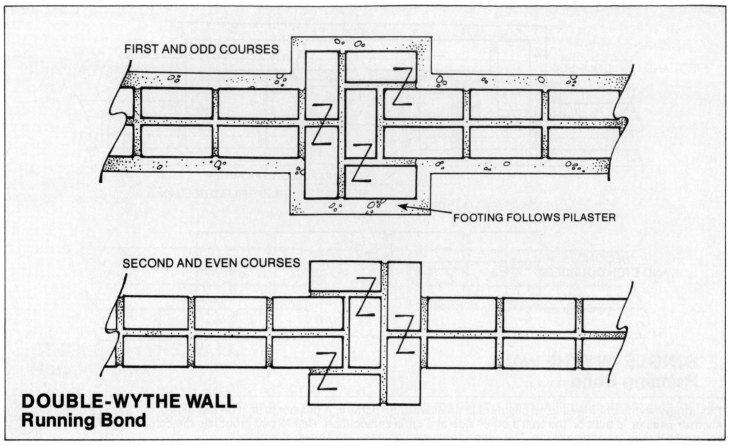

FIRST AND ODD COURSES

FOOTING FOLLOWS PILASTER

SECOND AND EVEN COURSES

DOUBLE-WYTHE WALL
Running Bond

Double-wythe wall with full pilaster on both sides. Wall is built in running-bond pattern. Z-bars are used for reinforcing. First and odd courses are shown at top. Second and even courses are at bottom.

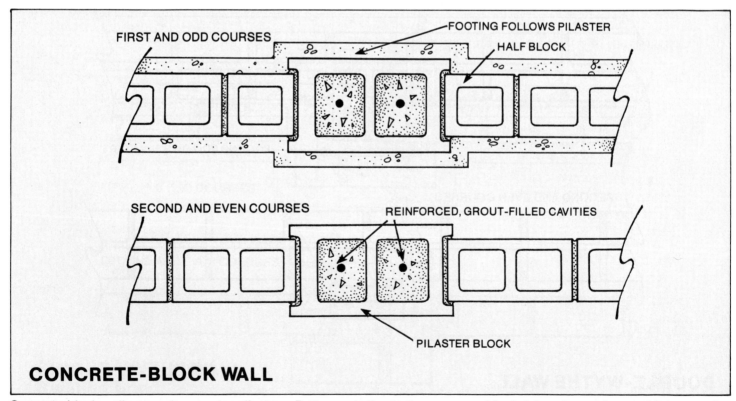

FIRST AND ODD COURSES

FOOTING FOLLOWS PILASTER

HALF BLOCK

SECOND AND EVEN COURSES

REINFORCED, GROUT-FILLED CAVITIES

PILASTER BLOCK

CONCRETE-BLOCK WALL

Concrete-block walls may also require pilasters. Patterns similar to the ones used for brick walls can be used for concrete-block walls. Half, full and alternating pilasters are common. This illustration shows special pilaster blocks used to reinforce a concrete-block wall. First and odd courses are shown at top. Second and even courses are shown at bottom. Reinforcing rod is used inside pilasters.

GLASS-BLOCK WALLS

The most practical and economical use of glass block for beginning builders is as small window sections in masonry walls.

Solid glass-block walls are excellent for noise reduction and security. Clear or textured blocks are popular. Other blocks are available to create reflective or prismatic effects and control glare or solar heat gain. Preassembled glass-block panels containing 20 blocks are available. These panels are set on wedges in a wall opening and mortared in place.

The installation instructions here are for windows containing 25 square feet or less. The dimensions for a window this size would measure approximately 5x5'. Glass-block windows or walls larger than 25 square feet should be built by experts.

Glass-block size should be choosen before you construct the masonry wall. Design the masonry wall opening so the glass blocks will fit in the opening. Glass-block sizes are nominal. Allow for 1/4-inch mortar joints between blocks. Glass blocks are available in the following standard sizes:

*3x6", *4x8", 6x6", *6x8", 8x8" and 12x12".

The glass-block sizes with an asterisk (*) can be used with 6- and 8-inch squares for flexibility in completing any size window. 4x12" and 12x12" sizes of blocks are also compatible.

Glass blocks are not *loadbearing,* which means they cannot carry or support weight. A glass-block wall or window will support a few courses of masonry. However, if you plan to position the panel with heavy masonry above it, a metal header must be installed.

Glass block is available in many attractive patterns and clear VUE ® blocks.

GLASS-BLOCK WINDOW

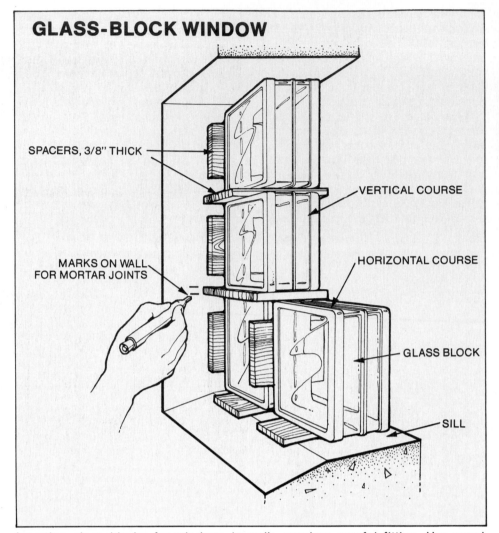

SPACERS, 3/8" THICK

VERTICAL COURSE

MARKS ON WALL
FOR MORTAR JOINTS

HORIZONTAL COURSE

GLASS BLOCK

SILL

Inserting glass blocks for windows in walls requires careful fitting. Use wood spacer block between blocks and the opening to simulate mortar joints. Mark location of mortar joints on wall opening.

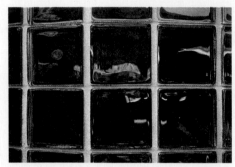

Mortar joints are usually struck or smoothed. Excess mortar should be cleaned from glass blocks before mortar dries.

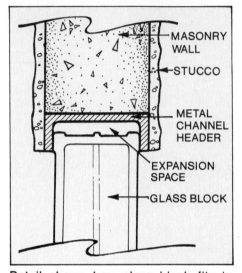

MASONRY WALL

STUCCO

METAL CHANNEL HEADER

EXPANSION SPACE

GLASS BLOCK

Detail shows how glass block fits in metal channel header for window opening in heavy masonry wall.

Level the windowsill first. If you have used careful building techniques, the windowsill opening in the masonry wall will be level. If the sill slopes to either side or the middle, the first bed of fresh mortar will level it out. The bed of mortar must be figured as part of the overall window opening measurement.

Glass blocks should be preplaced before actually mortaring them in place. This is called a *dry run*. Place loose block in each window opening to create one complete horizontal and one complete vertical row. Place 1/4-inch-thick wood spacers between the glass blocks to simulate mortar joints 1/4 inch thick. Make pencil check marks on the wall at the top and bottom of each spacer. These marks represent approximate mortar joint positions.

Setting the block in place without mortar allows adjustments to be made for a problem-free installation.

Installing glass blocks is easy. Put a layer of mortar on the windowsill. Smooth the mortar with a trowel to create an even bed. Put a layer of mortar on the side of the opening where the first block will butt against the wall. Put mortar on one vertical edge of each block at a time and place them in position against each other to create the first row.

Make sure the first row is level. Check it with a mason's or carpenter's level. Position each glass-block row so all mortar joints line up with the check marks on the wall. Apply a bed of mortar across the top of the first row of glass blocks. Make sure all spaces between the glass blocks are filled. Repeat the process for each new row until all blocks are mortared in place and the window is complete.

Glass blocks can move in the mortar as you position them. This movement is called *sinking* or *floating*.

Prevent sinking by mixing dryer mortar to create more substantial joints. Press tops of blocks with the trowel handle to align them.

Smooth mortar joints after the glass-block windows have set for approximately 2 hours or when the mortar is almost dry. Smooth all joints to remove excess mortar. This gives a clean, professional-looking job. The smoothing procedure compacts the mortar, creating a moisture-proof seal. Use a concave striking tool, called a *jointer*, to smooth the joints.

Clean glass block after mortar joints are firm. Wipe off excess mortar using a cloth and some water. Don't let excess mortar dry before attempting to clean the window surface. Dried mortar is difficult to remove. Do not use steel wool or other abrasive materials to remove partially dried mortar. These materials will scratch the glass.

Fieldstone rubble laid in random pattern with mortar.

DRY-STONE WALL

The two stone walls shown here require skill in composition to bring out the beauty of the material. Gravity and careful positioning of stones hold them in place.

Large stones are used in lower portions of each wall for stability and appearance. Smaller stones are placed near the top. Dry-stone walls should lean inward at a rate of 1 inch per foot of vertical height.

Stone walls should be built on a footing or solid foundation. A shallow trench filled with packed earth can serve as a solid base for dry-stone walls. See footing section, page 74.

Free-standing stone walls should not be higher than the thickness of the base. Height of dry-stone retaining walls should be equal to 1/2 the base thickness. Both walls shown on this page are built on shallow foundations. Because the stones are free to move, shifting due to frost heaving normally dislodges only a few small stones.

Low retaining wall is made from flagstone laid dry and coursed.

After the footing is prepared, the wall can be laid. Place large *bondstones* at each end of the wall and at regular intervals along the footing. Bondstones are stones that extend through the entire width of the wall. Bondstones help stabilize the wall and tie smaller stones on each side together.

Place the first course of stones in position between the bondstones. Use large stones in the first course and near the bottom of the wall. Place stones with the flat side down. Adjust position, size and shape of stones to avoid large gaps in the first course.

After the first course is in position, build up the ends of the wall. Place several stones at one end and adjust the position, size and shape until they fit together with little or no movement. Stones should be placed across the width of the wall and toward the center, interlocking them as they are positioned.

Use small stones to fill in gaps and holes between larger stones and in the middle of the wall. Repeat this building process at the other end of the wall. Gradually extend the placement of both large and small stones from the ends toward the center of the wall.

As stones are placed, each face of the wall should tilt or lean in toward the middle of the wall. Tilting the faces inward forces the weight of stones to rest against each other, helping to stabilize movement. Gradual tilting also makes the wall narrower at the top.

Continue placing stones across the wall's width and length until the desired height is reached.

Use the flattest and broadest stones for the top course of the wall. These large stones serve as a cap.

The low retaining wall on page 113 is built in the same basic manner as the free-standing wall. The exception is that the retaining wall is built against a wall of earth. The largest stones are placed at the base on a bed of gravel. Drainage tile is placed behind the wall as it is constructed. Each course of stones above the base is tilted back and down toward the earth.

Soil is placed between courses and packed around stones for extra stability and strength. The soil acts as a makeshift mortar, holding stones in position. Small plants grow in the soil, softening the shape of the stone wall.

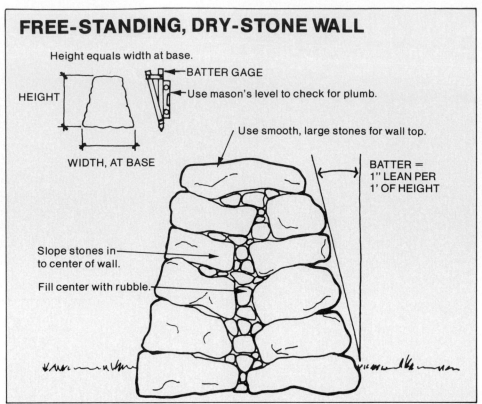

FREE-STANDING, DRY-STONE WALL

Height equals width at base.

HEIGHT

WIDTH, AT BASE

BATTER GAGE

Use mason's level to check for plumb.

Use smooth, large stones for wall top.

BATTER = 1" LEAN PER 1' OF HEIGHT

Slope stones in to center of wall.

Fill center with rubble.

Free-standing dry-stone wall is built in a shallow trench. Use large, flat stones for the base course. Height of wall should equal width of base. Use a batter gage to check the wall slope or batter. Hold the batter gage so board is plumb. If batter is 1 inch per foot and wall is 3 feet high, slant board 3 inches from vertical. Nail a board at 3-foot point to mark wall top.

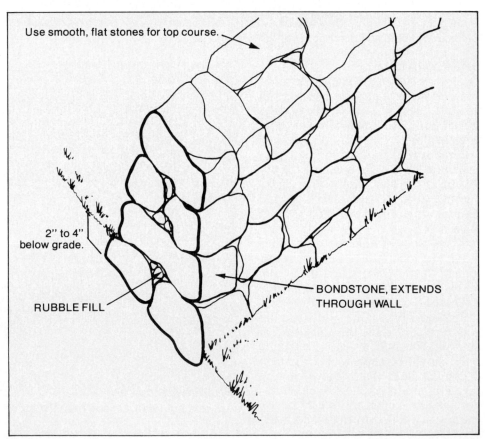

Use smooth, flat stones for top course.

2" to 4" below grade.

RUBBLE FILL

BONDSTONE, EXTENDS THROUGH WALL

Dry-stone wall requires use of bondstones to tie outer faces together. Place bondstone across both courses of the wall. Smooth, flat stones are used for top course.

HOW TO BUILD A MORTARED STONE WALL

Build a rock wall with mortar on a solid base or concrete footing. Stone must be clean and dry. Remove all dirt and debris. Pile stone in a variety of sizes near work area and mix mortar. This fieldstone rubble is being laid in random pattern. Lay base course first using largest available stones. Follow string guidelines. Base course is shown completed and coursework is progressing in sections from corner and end leads.

Mason's line is attached to a crude storyboard as a guide. Mason holds each rock in the course flush with guideline. The guideline indicates course level and batter or slope. Batter is adjusted as line is raised. An inward slope of 1 inch per 2 feet of height is recommended for mortared walls.

Mortar is applied to fill joints completely. Joints should be as narrow as possible. Try several different rocks in different positions to achieve the best fit before mortaring. Small stones and extra mortar fill holes in wall interior.

Wall construction progresses a section at a time. Joints must be struck before mortar hardens. Rake joints 1/2 to 3/4 inch deep with a dull, pointed stick. Rake joints when mortar is "fingerprint" hard. Excess mortar is brushed off with old broom. Complete each section and remove excess mortar before beginning work on the next section.

A GALLERY OF STONE WALLS

Rough-cut ashlar laid dry in random pattern.

Rough-cut ashlar laid dry and coursed.

Smooth-cut ashlar laid in mortar and coursed.

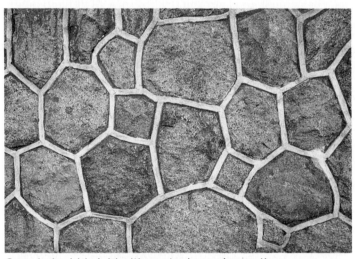

Quarried rubble laid with mortar in random pattern.

Fieldstone rubble laid dry in random pattern.

Dry-wall construction made from random fieldstones.

BROKEN-CONCRETE WALL

A wall of broken concrete can be an attractive garden feature. This wall is useful for changing levels in gardens. Broken-concrete walls are constructed in basically the same manner as the dry-stone wall described on page 113.

Large pieces of broken concrete, approximately 12 inches wide and 24 inches long, are easy to work with. Large pieces can be broken in smaller pieces as needed. Start the wall by preparing the footing.

Dig a shallow trench and place about 1/2 inch of sand in the bottom. The sand can be used as a leveling bed. Lay a footing of large pieces of broken concrete or make a footing of poured concrete. See page 74 for how to make a poured concrete footing.

After the footing is prepared, place the largest pieces of broken concrete at the base of the wall. These pieces form the first course of the wall. The thickness of the wall at the base should be equal to one-half the height. The height of broken-concrete and stone walls should be under 3 feet. The rest of the wall is built in the same manner as the dry-stone wall on page 113.

Moisture can seep out between course levels because no mortar is used. If the wall will be used as a terrace wall, place a layer of gravel or sand backfill behind it. If soil is placed between layers of concrete, small plants can be grown to soften the shape of the wall.

POURED-CONCRETE WALL

The smooth, clean lines of a poured-concrete wall adapt to both formal and informal landscapes. Concrete's fluid quality makes it versatile and strong. Concrete is easily formed in curves, straight lines or irregular shapes. Concrete walls are strong and durable, lasting years under the effects of weathering. Because of concrete's great strength, a wall doesn't need to be any wider than 8 inches. Examples of poured-concrete walls appear on pages 19 and 120.

The most important part of constructing a strong, attractive wall is to build strong, accurate forms. Building and aligning forms for poured-concrete walls is an exacting and time-consuming process. It takes more time to build forms than to pour and finish the wall. Forms must be strong enough to withstand the pressure exerted by the mass of dense, heavy concrete.

Precast-concrete planter in foreground provides contrast to broken-concrete wall behind. Precast concrete may be more economical than poured concrete for planters and low walls.

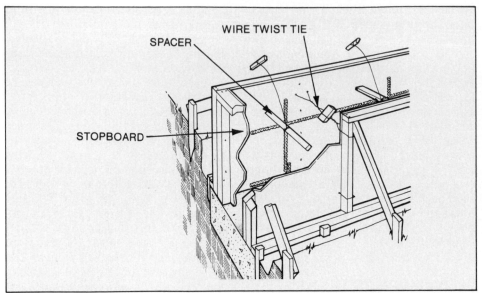

Use stopboards to close form ends. Twist ties draw wall form sides together to hold wood spacers in position. Spacer handles are held erect by stiff wire.

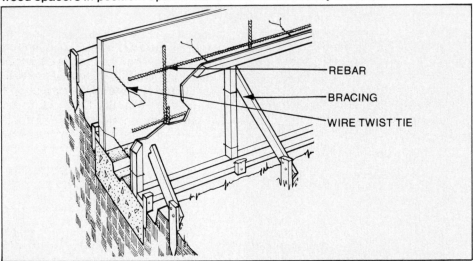

Build the wall form from plywood and stock lumber. Brace form securely. Wire ties are tightened later. Horizontal and vertical reinforcing bars are wired in place. Keep ends of rods at least 1-1/2 inches away from formwork and finished surfaces.

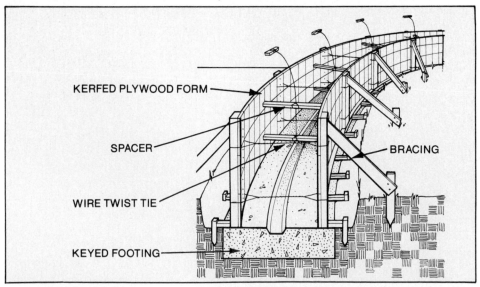

The method above is used for a curved wall. Make curved form using saw-kerfed plywood. Brace securely. Note key in footing.

Footings—Footings for concrete walls are usually twice as wide and as deep as the wall's width. See the illustration on page 74. Footings for concrete walls must be laid on a 6-inch-thick bed of gravel placed below the frost line. See page 74 for information on footing construction.

Building The Wall Form—A straight wall form is made from plywood sheets or *sheathing,* 2x4 studs, *spreaders* and *ties.* The sheathing—1/2-inch or 3/4-inch plywood and 3/4-inch-thick lumber—forms the sides of the mold.

Supporting the sheathing are 2x4 studs cut to length. The studs are placed vertically against the outside of the sheathing on 15-inch centers.

Spacers or spreaders are short pieces of 1x2 or 2x4 lumber. Spacers are cut to be as long as the wall is wide. Spacers are used to establish and maintain spacing between two sides of the form. They hold the sides of the form apart before concrete is poured. Long pieces of wire are attached to the spacers and placed over the top of the form. The wire allows you to remove the spacers after the concrete is poured. See the illustrations at left.

Ties are pieces of wire used to pull the sides of the form together. Small holes are drilled in the sides of the form at regular intervals. Wire ties are strung through the holes across the form. Use nails or small pieces of wood to hold the wire on each side of the form. See the illustration at left. The wires can be twisted to draw the sides of the form together. The wire ties are left in place during the pour. After concrete has set and forms removed, the ties are cut off flush with the wall surface.

Build the form centered on top of the footing. Measure and cut the plywood sheathing to the height of the wall. Nail the lengths of sheathing together with 1x4 wood cleats. Place the cleats on the outside of the form.

Make two sides for the form. Each side should be the length of the wall. Cut end pieces from plywood sheathing and nail the ends to each side. This makes a long, narrow rectangular box with no top or bottom.

To make forms for a curved concrete wall, cut *kerfs*—shallow saw cuts—in plywood sheathing or solid boards. Use a portable circular saw and cut the kerfs approximately 3/4 inch apart.

A simple spacing guide for kerfs can be made by driving two short nails into and slightly through a piece of scrap lumber. Drive the nails 3/4 inch away from the edge of the board. Cut the first kerf, then place the nail ends into the kerf, with the edge of the board 3/4 inch away. Place the saw against the guide and cut another kerf. Repeat the process until all kerf cuts have been made.

Soak wood before trying to bend it. Bend wood toward kerfs and build forms as described above.

Position spreaders and ties next. This is an important step. Spreaders and ties keep the sides of the form the same distance apart. This maintains the exact width of the wall.

When the wall forms are aligned, with spreaders and ties in position, the forms must be braced to prevent movement as the concrete is poured. Use 2x4 braces and nail them to 2x4 studs on the side of the form. Place braces at a 45° angle between the top of the studs and the ground. Drive a wooden stake in the ground at the end of the angled brace. Nail the brace to the stake. The stake keeps the form from lifting as concrete is poured.

After the form is braced, the wall

Many saw cuts partway through a board produce *kerfs*. Kerfed boards can be bent to create formwork for curved, poured-concrete walls.

reinforcing must be positioned inside the form. Concrete walls should be reinforced with 1/2-inch-steel reinforcing rods both vertically and horizontally. Vertical rods should be placed 5 feet apart and staggered on each side of the form. Vertical rods are wired to the reinforcing rods that

project from the footing. The horizontal rods are wired to the vertical rods approximately halfway up the wall. Keep horizontal rods a minimum of 4 inches away from the form sides. See the illustration on page 118. Reinforcing rods must be positioned to allow easy removal of wooden spacers.

Low walls define a gracious entry court by suggesting enclosure. Welcome breezes can still enter the garden.

Poured-concrete wall is stepped down sloping driveway. Wall is poured in sections. Control joints at each section prevent large cracks.

When the form is built, coat the inside with clean motor oil or a commercial releasing agent. The oil or releasing agent prevents concrete from sticking to form sides. This makes it easy to remove forms after concrete has set.

Long walls may require several pours of concrete. Divide the wall into several equal sections. Cut a *stopboard* to separate the pours. The stopboard is a board that fits between the sides of the form from top to bottom of the wall. The stopboard is held in position by cleats of scrap wood nailed to the inside of the form. The stopboard must not be removed until the concrete has hardened in a wall section. Short walls can be poured all at once. Long or tall walls may require several pours of concrete.

Mixing Or Buying Concrete—You can buy the separate ingredients for making concrete, purchase premixed ingredients or have *ready-mix* concrete delivered. Ready-mix concrete is premixed, ready-to-pour concrete.

The method you choose depends on the wall size, the number of helpers you have and the weather. If the weather is hot, you must work fast to keep concrete from setting up or hardening too fast. If you are mixing your own concrete, it helps to have one person mixing concrete. Another person can bring concrete from the mixer to the wall. Several people may be necessary to help pour the concrete.

Portable power mixers can be rented to mix concrete. Rent a mixer that holds at least 6 cubic feet of materials. It may be possible to pour concrete directly from the mixer into the form. If not, you will need a wheelbarrow to move concrete from the mixer to the form. If you have ready-mix concrete delivered, arrange for it to be poured directly into the form or have several wheelbarrows ready to move the concrete.

The basic formula for mixing your own concrete is:

1 part cement.
2-1/2 parts sand.
2-1/2 parts 3/4-inch stone and gravel aggregate.
1/2 part water.

If you use a shovel to measure ingredients, the following method will produce a good, strong concrete mix.

Place 6 shovels of concrete in the mixer. Add 14 shovels of sand and 14 shovels of stone or aggregate. Mix together until all ingredients are the same color. Add 3 quarts of water and mix until the concrete is fluid and slightly stiff. Add more water if the mixture is stiff and crumbly. Add a little cement, sand and aggregate if it is too fluid and runny.

Properly mixed concrete is slightly fluid, but packs together in a workable mass. It is easy to move and work into a smooth surface with a trowel.

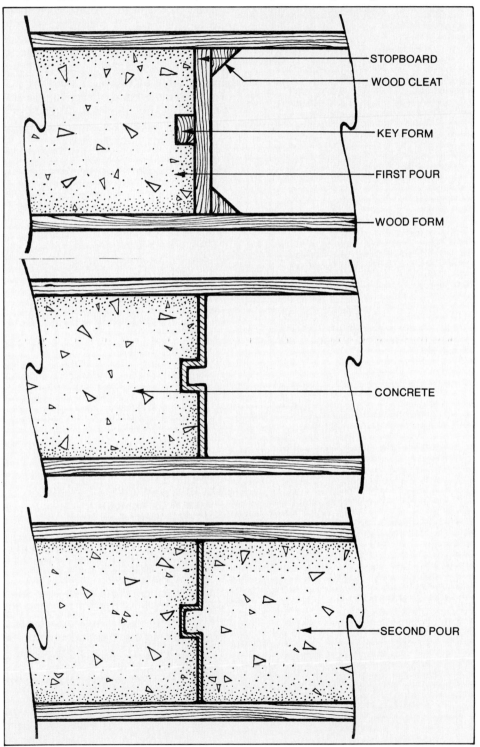

STOPBOARD
WOOD CLEAT
KEY FORM
FIRST POUR
WOOD FORM
CONCRETE
SECOND POUR

Bird's-eye view of poured-concrete wall shows keyed form on stopboard. Stopboard is used for long walls that require many pours. Key helps lock pours together.

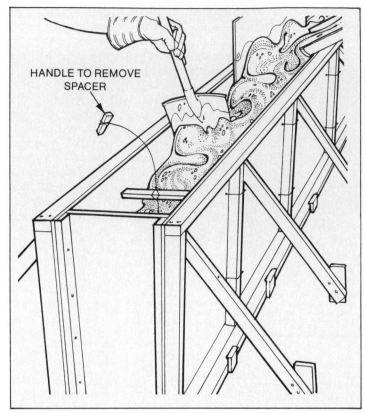

HANDLE TO REMOVE SPACER

Pour concrete in continuous layers 6 to 8 inches deep. Prod and tamp concrete with a shovel or 2x4. Agitate concrete next to form to force large aggregate away from surface. Note handles for removing wood spacers.

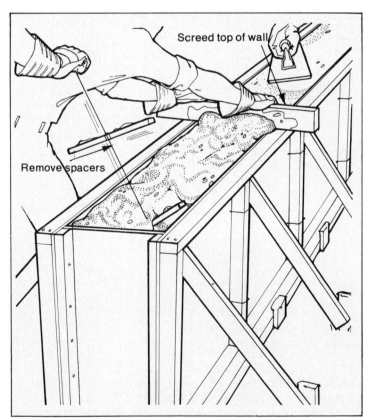

Screed top of wall

Remove spacers

Pull spacers and float or screed concrete on top of the wall. Screeding helps distribute concrete evenly, filling low spots and leveling high spots. It also produces a smooth finish.

To determine the amount of concrete needed for a wall, use the following method:

Figure the number of cubic feet in the wall. Multiply height in feet by length in feet by width in feet. This figure is the number of cubic feet contained in the wall. Round this figure up to the next 10 cubic feet. Divide this figure by 10. See the example below. Multiply this new number by the quantities of the ingredient listed in the table below. This will give you the amount needed of each ingredient. When figuring quantities of ready-mix concrete, remember that each cubic yard contains 27 cubic feet.

Wall height	3 feet
Wall length	28 feet
Wall width	8 inches or 2/3 foot

3 x 28 x 2/3 = 56 cubic feet. Round up to 60 cubic feet.

60 ÷ 10 = 6. The number 6 is the multiplier.

Cement	6 x 2.4 = 14.4 sacks of cement.
Sand	6 x 5.2 = 31.2 cubic feet of sand.
Gravel	6 x 7.2 = 43.2 cubic feet of gravel.
Ready-Mix	6 x .37 = 2.22 cubic yards or 59.9 cubic feet of ready-mix concrete.

Add 10% to these figures and round up to the next highest number to make sure you have enough materials. The final quantities needed are:

16 sacks of cement.

35 cubic feet of sand.

48 cubic feet of gravel.

2-1/2 cubic yards or 66 cubic feet of ready-mix concrete.

An *air-entraining agent* can be added to concrete. Air-entraining agents introduce tiny air bubbles into the concrete mix. These bubbles help the concrete expand and contract in areas subject to freezing and thawing weather conditions. A power mixer must be used to add air-entraining agents to concrete.

Pouring Concrete—Pour mixed concrete into the forms a little at a time. Pour concrete in continuous layers 6 to 8 inches deep. Tamp concrete in place with the end of a 2x4 or shovel.

Force concrete around the reinforcing rod. This tamping process helps eliminate air bubbles and moves concrete into open areas. Use a straight-blade shovel and agitate or move the concrete around next to the form sides. This agitation forces large aggregates away from the surface.

As concrete is poured in the form it will cover the spacer boards placed earlier. Remove spacer boards after they are covered with several inches of concrete by carefully pulling on the attached wires.

Continue tamping concrete, removing spacer boards and adding more concrete until the forms are filled. Make sure all spacer boards have been removed.

When the last layer of concrete has been added to the form, screed or *strike off* the top surface of the wall. Use a short piece of 2x4 lumber and drag it across the top of the form to smooth and remove excess concrete. This striking process may need to be done several times to remove all the excess concrete.

If the wall is being constructed in several pours, allow the first section to *set* or harden for at least 48 hours. The stopboard can be removed after 48 hours and another pour can be made.

Curing Concrete Walls—Poured concrete walls must be kept moist for four to seven days, depending on weather conditions, to *cure* properly. Curing is the process that ensures proper *hydration,* a chemical reaction of water and cement that produces hardened concrete. Curing gives strength to concrete. The wall should be covered with wet burlap or plastic sheeting to keep it from drying out.

When the wall has cured, forms can be removed. First, cut the tie wires to release the side walls of the form. Remove all external stakes and bracing. Carefully remove the cleats that joined the form sides together and pull forms off the wall. Trim protruding ends of tie wires as close to the wall as possible.

Allow the finished wall to set for several days before painting, applying stucco or veneer facing. Fill in dirt next to the wall as desired.

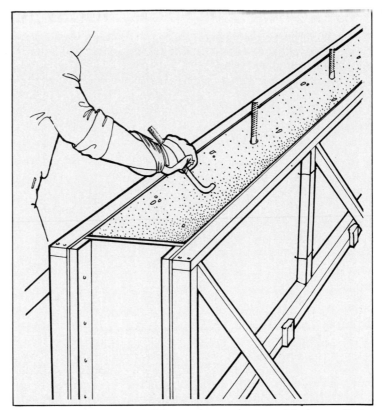

When concrete has stiffened slightly, insert J-bolts, called anchor bolts, to hold a wooden cap or seat. The wall top may be troweled to obtain a smooth finish. Use a steel trowel after water sheen has disappeared from the surface. Keep wall surface damp. Do not trowel the surface of a foundation wall.

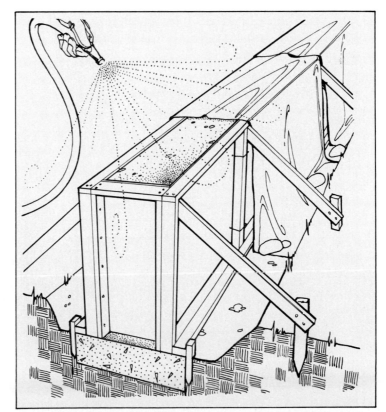

Leave wooden wall forms in place until curing process is complete. Cover wall with masonry sealer or plastic sheeting to prevent moisture loss. Allow wall to cure four to seven days.

IDEAS FOR LOW, POURED-CONCRETE WALLS

The illustrations on these two pages show four different ways poured-concrete walls can be used to enhance landscape settings. Each design provides for low maintenance around the wall and invites visitors to stop and relax.

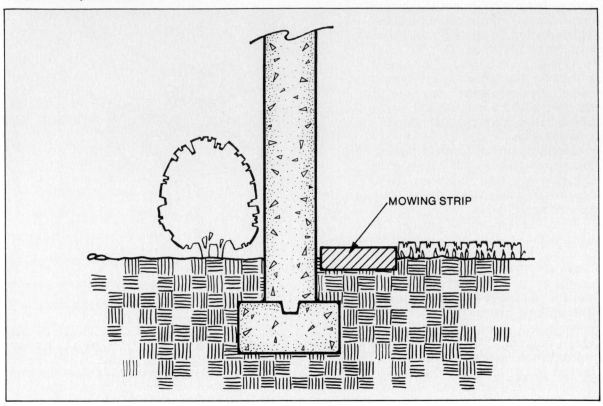

An 8-inch-wide mowing strip along edge of wall makes it easier to mow lawn. The mowing strip eliminates the need for hand trimming.

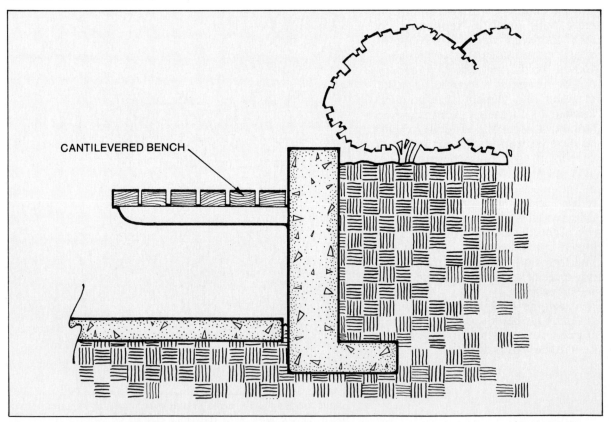

Bench cantilevered from a low, poured-concrete wall is easier to sweep under than bench on supports.

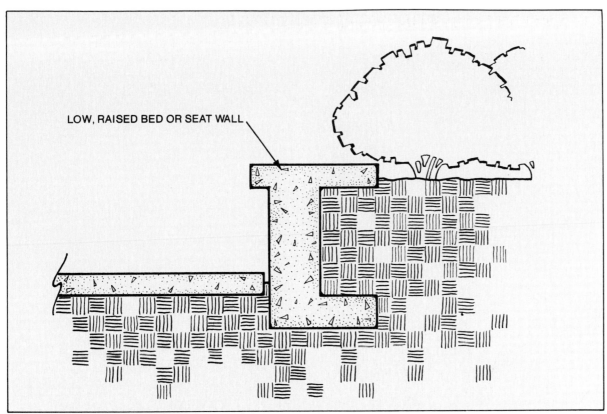

Use a low wall as a bench around the edge of the patio. Raising planting areas separate planting from paving. Area is easier to garden because bending and stooping is reduced.

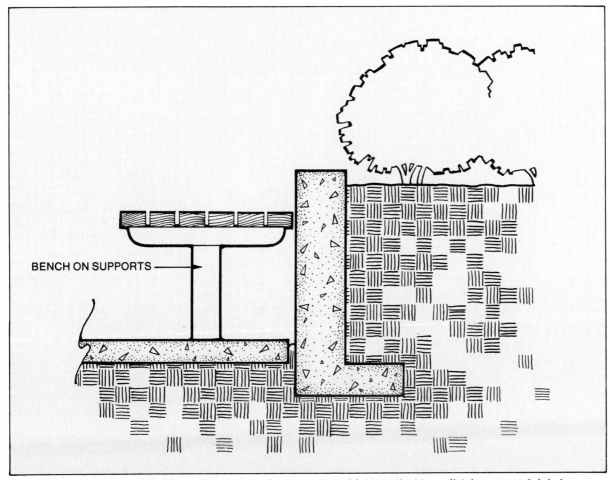

Bench on supports is difficult to sweep under. Legs create odd spots that trap dirt, leaves and debris.

Straight lines and textured surface of stucco wall are accented by sunlight in Southwestern setting. Stucco should be applied by experts.

STUCCO WALL

Stucco walls are beautiful and simple in appearance. They have special appeal in warm climates where the sun accents the textured surface.

A wide variety of textures are possible. Rough textures help conceal imperfections in a wall surface. Stucco is durable and long-lasting in most climates and can be applied over wood or masonry walls. Applying stucco finishes requires skill. It's not a job recommended for beginners.

Preparing Surfaces—The first step in applying stucco is to prepare the surface for the stucco. Wood-stud walls should be covered with 3/4-inch exterior-grade plywood sheathing, a layer of 30-pound *building paper* and chicken wire before the stucco is applied. Building paper is a heavy paper impregnated with asphalt to make it water-resistant.

On old masonry or adobe walls, nail 1-inch-mesh chicken wire to the wall surface with masonry nails. When stucco is applied to the wall, it adheres to the chicken-wire mesh.

New masonry walls should be clean and damp, but not wet. Spray the wall with water to dampen it just before applying the stucco. If the wall does not absorb the moisture, use a *bonding agent* to prepare the surface. A bonding agent serves as an attaching link between the masonry wall and the stucco coating.

A bonding agent can be mixed using this formula:

1 part portland cement.

1 or 2 parts sand.

Enough water to make a heavy, thick mixture.

The bonding agent should be the consistency of thick paint. Apply the bonding coat to the new masonry wall. Allow it to dry, then apply stucco as described below.

Applying Stucco—Stucco is applied with a trowel over prepared surfaces. Three layers are required over old surfaces. New masonry needs two layers.

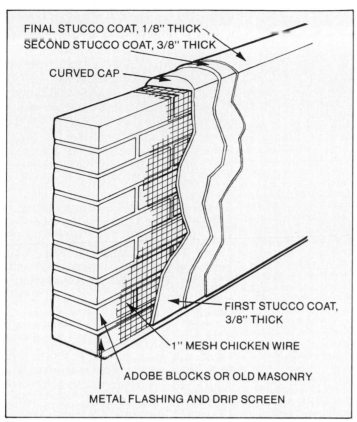

FINAL STUCCO COAT, 1/8" THICK
SECOND STUCCO COAT, 3/8" THICK
CURVED CAP
FIRST STUCCO COAT, 3/8" THICK
1" MESH CHICKEN WIRE
ADOBE BLOCKS OR OLD MASONRY
METAL FLASHING AND DRIP SCREEN

Stucco is an attractive covering for old, uneven walls. Applying stucco over rough or irregular surfaces, painted walls or adobe requires more surface preparation than new concrete-block walls.

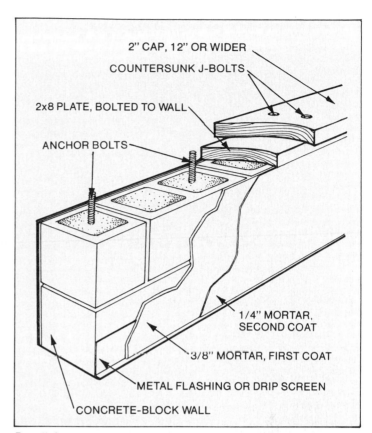

2" CAP, 12" OR WIDER
COUNTERSUNK J-BOLTS
2x8 PLATE, BOLTED TO WALL
ANCHOR BOLTS
1/4" MORTAR, SECOND COAT
3/8" MORTAR, FIRST COAT
METAL FLASHING OR DRIP SCREEN
CONCRETE-BLOCK WALL

Detail for stucco over new concrete-block wall. J-bolts or anchor bolts hold wooden cap. J-bolts are set in stiff grout in top course of wall. Plan the wall seat to be approximately 16 inches high.

Spread the first layer of stucco approximately 3/8 inch thick on the wall surface. While the stucco is still wet, score or scratch the surface. Scoring roughens the surface. This is called the *scratch coat.* Allow this coat to dry before applying the second coat of stucco.

The second coat should also be applied approximately 3/8 inch thick. Score the surface of the second coat of stucco and allow it to dry. Finally, apply the last coat of stucco approximately 1/8 inch thick.

Finishing Stucco Walls—The top of stucco walls should be covered with a cap to protect the top from moisture. Caps can be made from tile or bricks. Tile or brick caps are placed at an angle across the wall top. See illustration above. These caps add color and texture to the wall. Metal flashings can be attached to the top of tall walls.

Panel of rustic-wood spindles opens up courtyard to light, breeze and view. Smooth coat of colored stucco gives an adobe-look to this wall.

Low retaining wall of railroad ties defines edge between lawn and slope plantings.

TIMBER RETAINING WALLS

Rustic retaining walls are ideally suited to hillside gardens. The wall at left is constructed from used railroad ties. It has a rugged appearance.

Railroad ties are usually made from fir, redwood or oak. Ties are usually pressure-treated with creosote wood-preservative. They will last for years in contact with the ground. Railroad ties can be a bargain, but prices do vary. Railroad ties may not be as economical as regular timber.

New railroad ties usually measure 6 inches high by 8 inches wide by 8 feet long. Used railroad ties may vary in length because damaged ends may have been cut off. Buy dry railroad ties if possible. Wet creosote is sticky, smelly and harmful to plants. Select the straightest ties you can find.

Other large wooden posts and beams can be used in the garden. Old telephone poles, bridge supports and large fenceposts make good materials for walls. Lumberyards and do-it-yourself centers sell landscaping timbers manufactured for garden use.

These wooden materials can be used in different ways to construct unique walls. Telephone poles, large beams and railroad ties can be cut to length and laid horizontally for long walls. They can be cut and placed vertically to create a different look. Wooden materials can even be combined with masonry materials to create rustic-looking walls.

Cut these large wooden materials to size with a portable chain saw or a two-man handsaw. Wooden materials can be attached together with an assortment of fasteners. Large steel spikes, long bolts and lag screws can be used. See the fasteners section on page 150.

Timbers placed horizontally can have holes drilled through the ends. Extra-long wood-boring bits can be rented from rental companies. After holes are drilled, long bolts, steel reinforcing rods or pipe can be used to join timbers together. Pipes or reinforcing rods used in this manner should be driven slightly below the surface to avoid exposed sharp edges.

If wooden materials are used to make a retaining wall, place gravel backfill and perforated drain tile or drill weepholes behind the wall to allow for water drainage.

Follow the instructions on the next page to construct the wall shown above left.

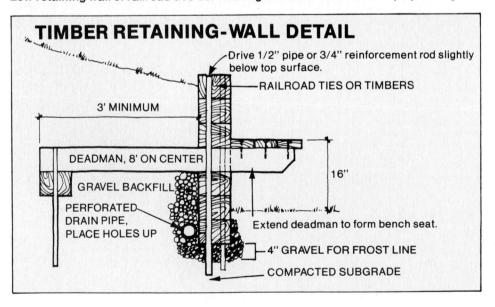

TIMBER RETAINING-WALL DETAIL

Drive 1/2" pipe or 3/4" reinforcement rod slightly below top surface.

RAILROAD TIES OR TIMBERS

3' MINIMUM

DEADMAN, 8' ON CENTER

GRAVEL BACKFILL

PERFORATED DRAIN PIPE, PLACE HOLES UP

16"

Extend deadman to form bench seat.

4" GRAVEL FOR FROST LINE

COMPACTED SUBGRADE

Determine the location of the retaining wall. Excavate soil for placement of ties and *deadmen* located 8 feet apart. Deadmen are large, heavy objects placed into soil behind retaining walls. Deadmen extend out from the bank of soil and into the wall structure. They help tie the wall structure to the soil bank to prevent movement. See the illustration, page 128.

Next, measure the length and height of the wall and determine how many railroad ties are needed. Use a chain saw to shorten railroad ties and deadmen if necessary.

Drill 1/2-inch holes through one end of each deadman. Position the deadmen into the soil bank. Place a 3-foot-long piece of 1/2-inch pipe through the hole and drive the pipe into the soil. This pipe anchors the deadman. Another method requires attaching a short cross piece to the buried end of each deadman.

Before laying the railroad ties, place a layer of gravel backfill and perforated drainage tile behind the wall's location to allow for drainage.

Lay the first course of railroad ties against the bottom of the soil bank, end to end. Place the next course of ties on top of the first course. Overlap the ends as much or as little as you want. Carefully position ties around the deadmen. Cut off ties with a chain saw if necessary.

Build up two or three courses, then drill 1/2-inch holes down through the railroad ties at regular intervals. Drill additional holes through the deadmen into the ties. Use an extra-long wood boring bit and a portable electric drill. The bit should be the same size as the fastener that will be used to join the ties together. A piece of 1/2-inch pipe was used for the wall shown.

After holes are drilled, place pieces of 1/2-inch pipe into the holes and drive the pipe down through the railroad ties. This pipe serves as a large nail and holds the ties together.

Lay another two or three courses of railroad ties. Remember to overlap the ends. Drill more holes and join the ties together with 1/2-inch pipe. Drive the ends of the pipe below the wood surface on the final course of the wall. Drilling the holes and driving the pipe is not easy. The process takes considerable time and effort, but the wall will be solid and secure for years.

Left: Drilling holes for drift pins or bars that tie timbers together requires heavy-duty drill and long, wood-boring bits. Note string guidelines to align wall top and excavated slope behind wall.

Below: Cutting timbers and railroad ties should be done with large circular saw or chain saw.

Steep slope was terraced using several low walls. As plantings mature, walls will be hidden by foliage.

4

HOW TO BUILD GATES

Above: Ornate metal gate is custom-crafted by expert iron worker. Design is unique and impressive in this showcase home landscape.

Left: Simple board gate is attached to brick pilaster with masonry hinges. Wooden gate strike is attached to opposite pilaster.

Gate Design

Gates can be designed to complement or contrast with a fence, wall or hedge. Gates have low visibility if constructed from the same materials as an adjoining fence. Gates with low visibility create privacy and help provide seclusion. Gates that contrast with adjoining walls or fences attract attention and invite visitors to enter.

Regardless of style or size, it is important that gates work properly. Gates should open and close without sticking or sagging.

When planning a gate, consider the amount of traffic and abuse the gate will receive. The type of posts, hinges and latch used depend on the size and weight of the gate. They must be carefully selected to work together for a well-functioning gate.

The fundamentals of gate construction are presented here. After the basic frame is constructed, the gate may be finished by adapting classic fence designs shown in this chapter.

The appearance of a gate is worthy of special attention. A little imaginative effort can create an attractive, inviting impression. A few special designs and building techniques follow the section on basic gate building.

ANATOMY OF A GATE

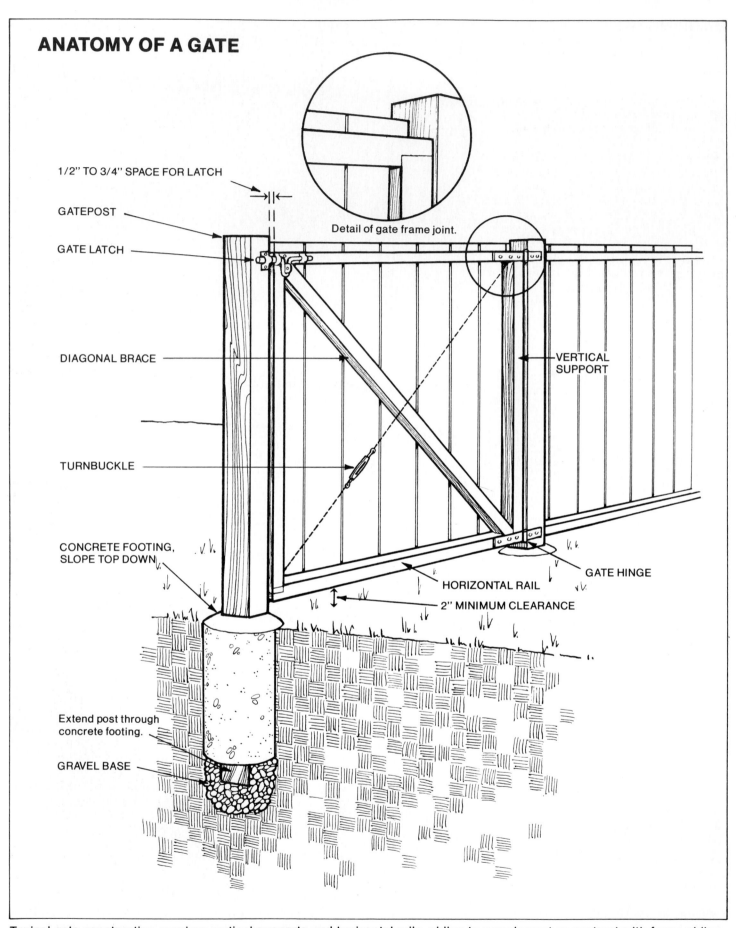

1/2" TO 3/4" SPACE FOR LATCH

GATEPOST

GATE LATCH

Detail of gate frame joint.

DIAGONAL BRACE

VERTICAL SUPPORT

TURNBUCKLE

CONCRETE FOOTING, SLOPE TOP DOWN

GATE HINGE

HORIZONTAL RAIL

2" MINIMUM CLEARANCE

Extend post through concrete footing.

GRAVEL BASE

Typical gate construction requires vertical supports and horizontal rails, siding to complement or contrast with fence siding, bracing and hardware items. Gateposts are also part of gate and fence structure.

GATE SIZE

The size of the gate is determined by its purpose and by the size of the fence or wall.

Height—Use a high gate for security. They are difficult to climb and create an imposing-looking obstacle. A high fence or wall looks better with a high gate.

Width—Gates should be made wide enough for two people to pass through, or one person with a wheelbarrow or lawnmower. The distance between gateposts determines actual gate dimensions. Gates should be at least 3 feet wide, unless they are seldom used. A single gate should not be wider than 4 feet. Gates 4 feet or more wide are difficult to support and tend to sag. If the opening is wider than 4 feet, use a gate with two sections.

Plan adequate side clearance to accommodate hinges and the latch. Usually 1/4-inch clearance is sufficient for most hinges. Latches require at least 1/2-inch clearance.

Sagging of oversize gates cannot be prevented by use of braces. Dividing a wide opening into two segments is the best idea.

Masonry hinges inserted in masonry wall support this beautiful wrought-iron gate.

Simple and sturdy wooden gate is made from 2x8 lumber framework, mitered at each corner. Inset is 1x12 pine.

HARDWARE

Choose latches and hinges first. It is best to design and build the gate to accommodate latches, hinges and the space between gateposts.

Gate Latches—Latches are used to keep gates closed. Several different types are available. They work in different ways.

Bolt Locks are often used as gate latches, but they are actually a lock. Bolt locks have a bolt that slides inside a sleeve. The sliding bolt end protrudes into a U-shaped metal bracket attached to the gatepost. The bolt assembly is attached to the gate.

Thumb Latches are functional and ornamental. The pressure of the thumb on a lever raises the strike bar from the catch. Thumb latches are available as a side-mounted assembly or a top mounted-assembly.

Universal Gate Latches are the most common type of latch. The latch is attached to the gatepost and the strike to the gate. The latch drops over the strike. The gate is opened by raising the latch off the strike.

Wooden Latches with sliding bars may be purchased or made in home workshops. Wooden latches work on the same principle as bolt locks, but they usually don't lock.

Popular self-latching-style gate latch is available in several designs. Latch pin serves as gate strike.

Bolt-action latch was constructed from threaded steel bars. It slides into a hole drilled in fence post. It can be operated from either side of gate.

This is typical U-shaped latch used on chain-link fence gates.

Wooden gate latch slides between gate and fencepost. Bent-iron straps hold wooden bar in place.

Deadbolt makes a secure lock for door gates. Use in low-traffic areas.

Loop latch secures gate to round post. Construction is typical of post-and-rail fences made from kits that include mortised poles.

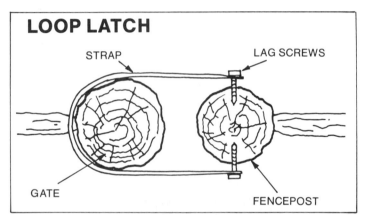

LOOP LATCH

STRAP

LAG SCREWS

GATE

FENCEPOST

A loop latch is used for gates with round structural elements. Lag screws hold latch strap to wood fencepost. Strap swings up and down on lag screws.

Metal hook-and-eye latch is useful for holding gate closed. This type of latch provides little security.

Canebolt slips into slot in paving to hold gate open or closed. When bolt is hooked into raised position, gate swings free.

Gate Hinges—Hinges must be heavy enough to support the gate's weight and withstand frequent use. Attaching screws or bolts must be large and strong enough to hold hinges to the gate. Three hinges are better than two for most gates. Heavy gates may require four hinges.

Use hinges with weather-resistant cadmium, zinc or galvanized coatings. Aluminum or brass hinges are durable and rust-resistant. Hinges can also be painted to reduce rust.

There are four basic types of hinges used on gates. They are available in several sizes and shapes.

Bolt-Hook-And-Eye Hinges consist of two parts, a leaf with an eye, and a bolt hook. The bolt hook is L-shape with a lag screw or nut-and-bolt end for attaching it to the gatepost. The leaf is bolted to the gate and fits down over the bolt hook. The gate can be lifted off the bolt hook.

Butt Hinges are used on gates and doors. The heavier the gate, the larger the hinge. Butt hinges have two leaves joined with a hinge pin at the center. Both leaves are attached flush or recessed on the gate and gatepost with wood screws or bolts.

T-Hinges are shaped like the letter T. They are attached flush on the gate and gatepost with bolts. T-hinges have two leaves joined with a hinge pin. The hinge's short side is bolted to the gatepost, the long side to the gate.

Strap Hinges have two equal-length leaves joined at the center with a hinge pin. Strap hinges are bolted flush with the gate and gatepost.

Bolt-hook-and-eye hinge is one of the strongest hinge types. Bolt extends completely through post.

Plain butt hinges are used on lightweight gates and doors.

Strap hinges are strong. Use them for heavy gates. Bolts attach hinge to gate and fencepost.

T-hinge is another excellent hinge design.

POST INSTALLATION

Wooden or metal posts must be installed securely in the ground to withstand the weight and pull of the gate. A general rule is to set 1/3 of the post in the ground. Minimum depth for a low gatepost is 18 inches. For a 6-foot gate, use 9-foot 4x4 or 6x6 wooden posts and secure them in a concrete collar.

Make sure posts are the same distance apart at top and bottom. Posts must be vertical. Use decay-resistant or pressure-treated wooden posts, or painted metal posts.

Gates for masonry walls or columns can be hung from hardware placed in mortar joints as the wall was built. If hardware is not already installed, drill holes in the wall for lead shields and expansion bolts. Use a portable electric drill and a carbide-tipped masonry bit to drill holes. Lead shields are inserted in the holes. When a bolt is screwed in a shield, the shield expands and securely holds the bolt. A board is secured to the wall with these bolts. Gate hinges are attached to the board.

This gate spring is standard gate hardware. It pulls gate shut automatically.

Gateposts and fenceposts must be installed securely in the ground. Set gateposts extra deep to withstand weight of gate.

Variation on the bolt-hook-and-eye hinge is shown here. Hook for gate hinge is attached to wood post with lag screws.

Expansion bolts hold gate hardware to masonry surfaces. Expansion bolts can also be inserted into mortar joints between bricks or blocks.

How To Build Gates   **137**

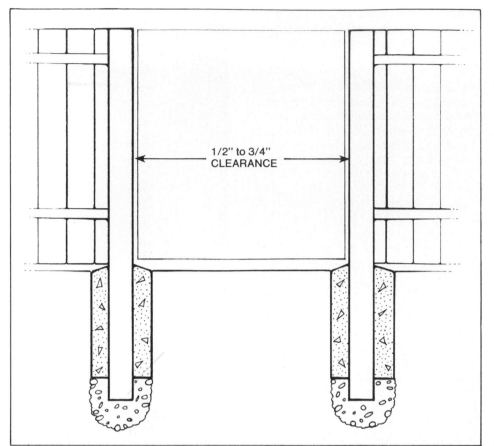

1/2" to 3/4"
CLEARANCE

Gates need securely anchored posts. Measure gate opening at top and bottom. If the gate opening is out of plumb, make minor adjustments in gate frame. Allow 1/2- to 3/4-inch clearance between gatepost and gate frame for latch. Leave 1/2-inch hinge clearance.

BASIC GATE FRAME

After gateposts have been set, carefully measure the distance between them. The distance should be the same at the top and bottom. Subtract 3/4 inch from this measurement to allow for hinges and latch. This is the gate's finished width.

Cut two 2x4s, or lumber of your choice, to this length. These two pieces are the horizontal gate rails.

Measure the vertical distance between the fence rails and cut two more 2x4s to this length. These boards are vertical uprights for the gate sides.

Nail the two uprights and two rails together to form a square or rectangle. Use butt joints or half-lap joints. See page 44 for details on woodworking joints. Use a carpenter's square to make sure all corners form 90° angles. This basic structure forms the gate framework.

Bracing keeps gates from sagging. A simple diagonal brace can be made from a 2x4. The brace should extend from the *bottom* of the hinge side to the *top* of the latch side. This placement supports the frame and counter-

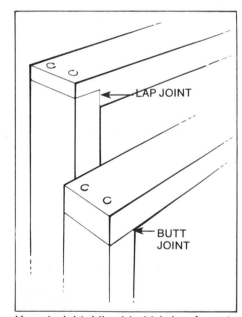

LAP JOINT

BUTT JOINT

Use straight, kiln-dried lumber for gate construction. Cut corners square or to adjusted angle on all framing members. Gates can be made with 2x4s laid flat—shown here with butt and lap joints—or on edge. Gate rails should align with fence rails. Gate made with rails on edge is stronger and produces a thinner gate.

Wide gate of heavy timbers is difficult to brace in conventional manner. Chain is attached to extended hinge post to reduce sagging. Turnbuckle at top of post may be tightened to take up chain slack.

acts sagging. Adding this diagonal brace increases the gate's strength. A 2x4 brace in the opposite direction does nothing to support the gate. Placing a brace from the top of the hinge side to the bottom of the latch side is a common mistake when building gates.

To make the brace, lay the basic gate frame on a level surface. Place a 2x4 diagonally from the top corner of the latch side to the bottom corner of the hinge side. Mark the 2x4 brace with angled ends to fit inside the frame.

Cut the brace ends with a hand saw or portable electric saw. Use wood screws or nails to attach the brace inside the gate frame. Use a carpenter's square and make sure the gate frame is square before you attach the brace.

Wire and a turnbuckle may be used instead of diagonal bracing. If using wire and a turnbuckle, the wire is strung from the *upper* hinge side to the *lower* latch side. Use eyehooks to attach the wire to the gate frame. The turnbuckle is placed in the middle of the wire. The turnbuckle may be adjusted at anytime necessary.

Turnbuckle is effective method of preventing gate from sagging. Attach turnbuckle with wire strung from upper hinge side down to lower latch side of gate. This is opposite to brace placement.

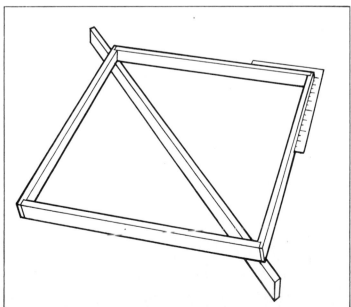

Place framing elements on a flat surface or work table. Square all corners and nail together. Lay a 2x4 diagonally from *bottom* of hinge side to *top* of latch side. Pencil in cutting marks. Cut brace piece for a tight fit. Nail brace to horizontal and vertical members of frame at both ends.

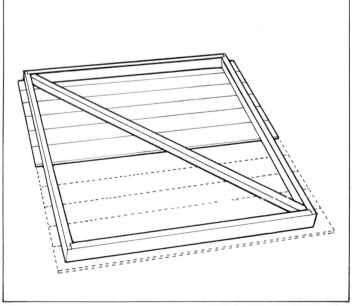

Attach siding to the gate frame. Make sure the gate is square. Lay out and mark spacing of siding on framework. Start attaching siding at hinge side.

Fit the gate. Hold gate in place, leaving space for hinges. Check to be sure gate fits and swings properly, without hitting posts. Trim frame as necessary so gate swings freely between posts.

Next, attach gate siding to the gate frame with galvanized nails. Siding can match the fence or complement a wall. Attach siding to gate rails in the same position as the fence siding. Position hinges on the frame and attach with wood screws or bolts.

HANGING THE GATE

Hanging or attaching a gate to a gate-post is usually the most difficult step.

The first step is to place the gate on wooden scraps in the gate opening. Adjust gate to the desired height as necessary. The gate bottom should be aligned with the fence bottom.

If you want the gate to open inward or the latch on the inside, align the back of the gate frame with the back of the gatepost. If the gate opens outward or the latch is on the outside, align the front of the gate with the front of the gatepost.

Position gate hinges on the gatepost and gate and mark the location of the *bottom* of the top hinge. Mark the screw or bolt holes. Drill *pilot* or guide holes in the post and gate for screws or bolts. Attach the top hinge. Make sure you leave support blocks in place under the gate. Repeat the procedure for the bottom hinge. Then attach other hinges.

Position and attach the latch on the gate. Then position the latch striker on the opposite gatepost.

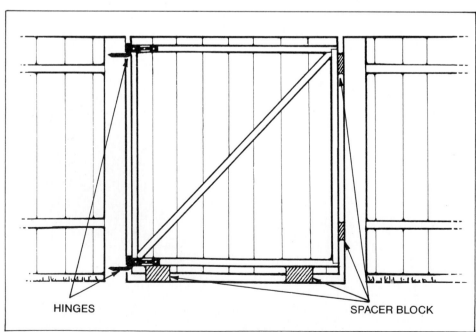

HINGES   SPACER BLOCK

Prop gate in place with wooden blocks on sides and at bottom. Attach loose ends of hinges to the post.

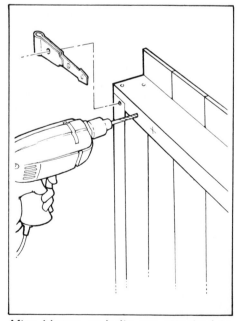

After hinges or bolts are attached to the gatepost, attach hinges to the gate framework. Use wood screws to attach hinges. Predrill screw holes with drill bit sized for wood screws being used.

GATE STRIKE DETAILS

Attach latch striker to gate using long screws or bolts. Then attach latch to gatepost.

This gate strike is attached to the gate. Gate strikes prevent gates from swinging past the gatepost.

This gate strike is attached to the post and painted to match.

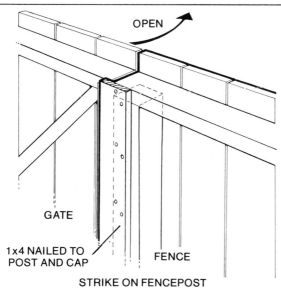

OPEN

GATE

1x4 NAILED TO POST AND CAP

FENCE

STRIKE ON FENCEPOST

This wooden gate strike is attached inside the fence-post. It is used for a gate that swings out.

OPEN

GATE

2x2 NAILED TO OUTSIDE OF POST AND TOP RAIL

FENCE

STRIKE ON FENCEPOST

This strike is for gates with framework elements laid on edge. The strike is attached to the fencepost. This style strike is popular for use with gates in masonry walls.

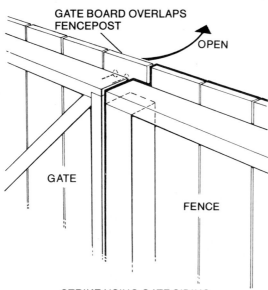

GATE BOARD OVERLAPS FENCEPOST

OPEN

GATE

FENCE

STRIKE USING GATE SIDING

This strike is used for a gate that swings out. It is made by extending board siding on the edge of the gate.

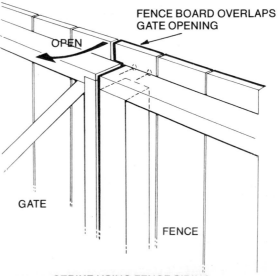

FENCE BOARD OVERLAPS GATE OPENING

OPEN

GATE

FENCE

STRIKE USING FENCE SIDING

This strike is made for a gate that swings in. It is made by extending board siding on the fence.

DIAGONAL BOARD GATE

Simple design and structural strength make this gate successful. The fence opening is filled with two panels. One panel is fixed, the other panel is the gate. When the gate is closed, the two panels look identical.

Openings in the gate allow light and viewing through each side. The diagonal pattern of the boards creates a contrast to the solid plywood fence. The diagonal siding serves as bracing. It runs from the top of the latch side to the bottom of the hinge side and keeps the gate from sagging.

Materials for this gate include 4x4 gateposts set in concrete, a framework of 1x6s, a 2x6 cap, 1x4 diagonal boards and a small amount of scrap lumber for blocking.

The 1x4 diagonals are sandwiched between a 1x6 framework. This placement makes the gate appear the same from both sides. A simple sliding bar latch is installed in the 1x6 framework. Common gate hinges are used for the gate.

Attractive gate needs no bracing because diagonal members keep gate from sagging. Gate frames covered with solid piece of plywood siding seldom require additional bracing.

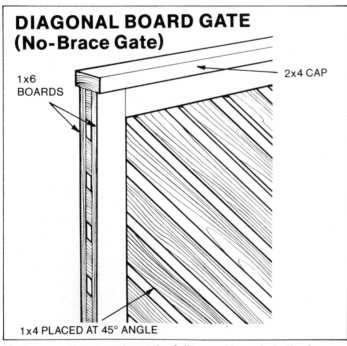

No-brace gate uses strength of diagonal boards in the framework to support gate structure and prevent sagging. Diagonal pattern is attractive and can provide contrast to fence siding.

Gate and matching fence panel form a chevron pattern. Gate is set in a dramatic, large-scale fence made of grooved plywood siding. Hinges are bolt-hook-and-eye type.

Closed pedestrian gate and driveway gate give this fence a solid look. Pedestrian gate doorknob is located to right of the light-colored slat.

Both gates open for access to extra off-street parking.

HIDDEN DRIVEWAY GATE

This seldom-used driveway gate has been carefully disguised as a fence. Details are carried across from the adjacent fence, shown on page 65. A pedestrian gate is provided for access to the front door.

When pedestrian and driveway gates are open, a 10-foot-wide access is created to the yard. The driveway gate consists of a two-part, double-hinged section that folds at the center. The driveway gate opens toward the street. The pedestrian gate opens toward the house.

Each gate section is held closed by a heavy cane bolt. A wire and turnbuckle provide bracing. The gate opening is framed by 6x6 posts. The framework uses 2x4 and 2x6 lumber. A 2x6 caps the gate. The 1x1 and 1x2 boards are nailed vertically to the framework. A steel gate strike and stop is bolted to the gate frame where the pedestrian gate meets the driveway gate.

Open pedestrian gate creates inviting entry. Closed auto gate appears to be solid fence.

When this hidden gate is closed, it resembles a hedge. Vines must be carefully trimmed to keep the gate swinging free.

Hidden gate in seldom-used garden area provides access but is completely concealed by vines.

DOOR GATES

The designs on these two pages illustrate the use of ordinary exterior doors as entrances to garden courtyards or garden rooms. These doors are modified by cutting openings in them or attaching moldings. The gates are hung on posts with standard door hinges. Locks or deadbolts are installed for security.

Striking gate design uses two standard doors. Door top is cut at an angle and faced with molding. Doors are covered with same siding material as fence.

Doorlike gate fills arch formed by wooden arbor.

Matching pair of door gates with cut-out panels permits a glimpse into garden. Thumb latch is standard gate hardware.

Two-part Dutch-door gate to sideyard was custom-made. Siding matches wall-like fence extension of house.

Simple, elegant gate is made from two standard doors painted white. Butt hinges and standard door latch are used.

Solid door panels contrast with open lattice fence. Decorative bell adds touch of elegance to entry.

BASIC BUILDING TERMINOLOGY

5

A

Adobe—A masonry block made with clay soils. Adobe is common throughout the Southwest.

Clay is mixed with straw, formed into blocks and dried in the sun or fired in a kiln. This ancient masonry material is best used in arid and semi-arid climates. Rain can ruin adobe. Adobe is often coated with stucco or a masonry sealer to protect it.

Steel reinforcing is essential for adobe walls in earthquake country and for walls more than 2 feet high. A solid footing or foundation is necessary. Pilasters are recommended to provide strength for one-wythe walls more than 30 inches high.

Block sizes vary. Long, thin blocks are popular. Modern adobe block is available with asphalt-based stabilizers added to reduce weathering effects.

Adobe blocks are heavy. The weight makes them expensive to transport out of the manufacturing region. *Slump stone* is a concrete-block product similar in appearance to adobe.

Aggregate—Hard gravel materials mixed with cement, sand and water to form concrete. Fine aggregate contains gravel pieces 1/4 inch or smaller. Coarse aggregate contains gravel pieces larger than 1/4 inch in size.

Air-Entrained Concrete—Concrete that contains millions of tiny air bubbles. The air bubbles improve the workability of concrete and increase concrete's resistance to freezing and thawing.

Air-Entraining Agent—An ingredient added to concrete or mortar to produce millions of tiny air bubbles. These bubbles are distributed evenly throughout the concrete mixture. See

air-entrained concrete. Air-entraining agents must be added to concrete with a power mixer.

Arbor—A wooden structure covered with shrubs or vines to shade an area.

Ashlar—A type of cut stone for building solid walls. Sometimes used to face a wall. Ashlar stones are cut into rough or smooth squares and rectangles. Ashlar is also a name for masonry made of squared stone laid in a random or a coursed pattern. This is called *coursed ashlar.*

Auger—A hand or machine-operated tool with a screwlike shank for boring holes in soil.

B

Backfill—Process of placing fill soil in construction. The soil used as fill.

Barbed Wire—A strong wire used for fencing. Barbed wire is made by twist-

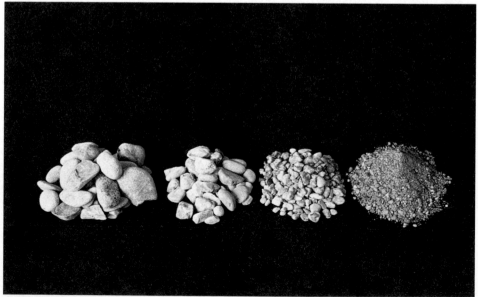

Natural adobe is made of clay soil and straw. Mixture is baked in the sun until blocks are firm. Stucco and mud plaster can be used to cover the surface to protect blocks from moisture.

Various sizes of gravel are mixed to form *aggregate,* one component of concrete. From left to right: 3/4-inch gravel, 1/2-inch gravel, pea gravel and coarse sand.

ing two or three strands of wire together. Sharp barbs are inserted at regular intervals.

Batten—A thin strip of lumber used to seal or strengthen a joint. Combined with boards for board-and-batten fencing.

Batter Boards—Boards placed at the corners of structures to serve as reference points. Batter board placement is essential for building straight walls with square corners. Batter boards hold a string guideline securely in position. See page 78 for information.

Batter Gage—An instrument used to check walls for comformity to specified pitch or slope.

Bed Joint—The mortar joint in masonry walls that runs horizontally. It serves as the bed or mortar base for masonry units.

Benderboards—Thin, narrow boards that are easily bent into curved shapes. Used for making edge forms for curved walls, landscaping edges and sidewalks. Usually made from plywood or laminated hardboard.

Bleach—See fence finishes, page 49.

Block And Tackle—An arrangement of one or more pulley blocks, with rope or cables, to make a pulley system. Block and tackle is used to stretch wire for fencing.

Blocking—A method for supporting horizontal members such as fence rails. Nail wood blocks to posts, then nail rails on the blocks. See page 44.

Bond—Interlocking method of the pattern made by brick or block units in a masonry wall. Also means the adhesion between mortar and units.

Bond-Beam Block—Concrete block made for horizontal reinforcing.

Bondstones—Large stones placed across the width of walls during construction. Bondstones *bond*, or hold and tie the two outer faces of walls together. See page 114.

Brick—A masonry building unit made from clay and molded into oblong blocks. The clay blocks are *fired* or baked in a *kiln*, a large oven.

Building Codes—Legal restrictions imposed by local governments on construction of buildings, methods and materials used in construction.

Butter—Using a trowel to apply mortar to block, brick or other masonry units.

Butt Joint—A construction joint formed by placing two boards, bricks or blocks end to end or edge to edge.

C

Cane Bolt—A latch attached to the bottom of a gate or door to hold the gate open or closed. Consists of a pin or bolt on the gate that slides into a hole or sleeve in the paving.

Caps—Wood, metal or stone materials placed along the top of fences or walls. Caps provide a finished look and reduce water penetration into the ends of boards, posts or mortar joints.

Carpenter's Level—A tool used by carpenters and masons to check for horizontal level and vertical plumb. Carpenter's levels are made of a length of wood or metal. Sealed glass vials of liquid with an air bubble trapped inside are placed in the frame. When an air bubble trapped inside the vial is centered, the object being checked is horizontally level or vertically plumb.

Cavity Wall—A wall that is hollow in the center. The center may be filled with mortar, grout, rubble or concrete.

Cement, Portland Cement—A binding agent that joins masonry materials into a solid unit.

Cement is a powdered blend of burned lime, silica, alumina and iron compounds. Cement mixed with water produces a chemical reaction called *hydration*. Hydration gives cement adhesive properties and produces hardened concrete.

Cement is a component of concrete and mortar. Cement combined with water, sand and aggregate, makes concrete. Cement mixed with additional lime, sand and water makes mortar. Cement can be combined with epoxy or latex to make patching compounds.

Chain-Link Fence—A metal fence material manufactured with interlocking wire mesh. Chain-link fencing material is durable and strong. See page 50 and 51 for installation instructions.

Clay, Clay Soils—Fine-grained soils composed of hydrous aluminum-silicate minerals. Clay soils are produced by the chemical decomposition of rocks and fine rock particles in water.

Clay soils have a sticky consistency and are difficult to excavate. Heavy clays are unstable on slopes when wet. Clay soils make adobe blocks if mixed with straw and dried in the sun or a kiln. Consult an engineer if you are considering building a retaining wall to hold steep slopes of clay soil.

Closure—Last masonry unit used to finish or *close* a course.

Collar—See *concrete collar*.

Collar Joint—Masonry wall mortar joint running vertically and horizontally between wythes. Usually reinforced with ties to hold two wythes together.

Columns—Slender, upright supporting structures that consist of a base, shaft and cap or *capital*. Columns may be free-standing or part of a wall. They are usually placed at the end of walls to help support gates. See pilaster, page 121.

Compacted Subgrade—The below-ground-level surface that is thoroughly tamped down to prevent soil from settling. A compacted subgrade provides a firm base for footings or foundations.

Concrete—A building material made of cement, sand and gravel aggregates and water. Concrete is composed of approximately 7% to 13% cement, 14% to 20% water and 60% to 80% aggregate. See page 121 for information on mixing and ordering concrete.

Concrete Collar—A ring of concrete placed around posts to securely anchor them. The bottom of the posthole is filled with gravel. The post base rests in gravel and not in a sealed concrete pocket. Concrete is poured around post sides and the hole is filled to the top. The hole sides are used as a form. Concrete is sloped away from post sides to shed water.

Control Joints—Joints placed in poured-concrete walls to form planes of weakness. Control joints reduce random crack forming because of drying shrinkage. Control joints are also used in concrete-block or brick walls to control the direction of cracks.

Countersink—To set the heads of nails or screws flush or below the surface.

Coursed Ashlar—Rough or smooth, square-cut stone laid in courses or layers to form a masonry wall. See *ashlar*.

Courses—Continuous, horizontal layers of building units, usually brick, concrete block or stone. Courses may also be constructed from railroad ties or wooden blocks.

Courtyards—A space enclosed by walls. Courtyards may be free-standing or attached to buildings or other walls.

Curing—The process of keeping concrete moist for a period of time after it has been poured.

Curing ensures proper *hydration,* a process that allows cement in concrete to react with water and harden. Strength, resistance to freezing and thawing damage, watertightness and wear resistance is gained if absorption and reaction with water proceeds slowly.

The amount of curing time varies depending on type of cement, mix proportions, required strength, weather and other factors.

Use the information provided here as a guide for curing times.
- Mortar and grout in unit masonry walls: four days—mist with water.
- Stucco: four days—mist with water.
- Concrete footings and low walls: four days minimum, seven days optimum.
- Substantial concrete walls: seven days minimum.

Curve—A line having no straight part. A bend having no angular part. Fences and walls are often built with curves to serve practical and aesthetic purposes. The feature section below describes how to plan and lay out curves in fences or walls.

Custom-Milled—Materials manufactured to customer specifications. Wooden fence and gate elements are often custom-milled by a cabinetmaker or woodworker. Fancy pickets, finials, ornamental post tops or turned spindles may be custom-milled.

Cut And Fill—The digging of soil or dirt from one location, the *cut,* and moving and placing the soil in another location, the *fill.* The cut is usually taken from a high spot to fill a low spot. This creates a smooth or level surface. The cut-and-fill procedure is used when building retaining walls to terrace a sloping site.

D

Dado—Rectangular groove cut to accept a rectangular element. Fenceposts may be dadoed to accept rails.

Deadman, Deadmen—A large, heavy timber or rock used to anchor a retaining wall to a soil bank. Deadmen are placed deep in soil and attach to the wall unit. The heavy weight and position tie the two units together.

Decks—Wood platforms located above ground and supported on posts. Fences and screens can be attached to existing decks by using *metal post anchors.* See *fasteners.*

Drainage—The process or method of draining water away from an area. Drainage systems are used for removing excess water from retaining walls.

HOW TO CURE CONCRETE

Concrete is cured by keeping it moist while it hardens. Keep concrete wet by sprinkling water on a covering of damp burlap or newspaper. Concrete can also be covered with plastic, waterproof building paper or a commercial spray-on product available from masonry suppliers. Wooden formworks protect the sides of concrete walls from too-rapid evaporation.

High temperatures accelerate evaporation. Evaporation interrupts hydration and produces a weak concrete or mortar. Be sure to sprinkle and mist exposed surfaces and formwork regularly during warm weather. Low temperatures retard the curing process. Concrete should not be poured when temperatures are near or below 32F (0C).

How To Plan A Curved Fence Or Wall

The first step in planning a curved fence or wall is to study your landscape and determine the structure's location. Follow the procedure described here to plot the curve's points in the landscape.

Attractive retaining wall is made from railroad ties. Ties are placed on end and sunk in ground. Curves emphasize natural landscape.

LAYING OUT CURVES

To plot a curve, scribe an arc in the landscape. Use a tightly stretched line as a giant compass.

Step 1. Locate and place a stake at each end point of the proposed structure.

Step 2. Stretch a string between the stakes. Locate the string's midpoint and mark it with a third stake.

Step 3. Tie a string to this middle stake. Stretch the string perpendicular or 90° to the first string.

Step 4. Anchor the end of this string with a fourth stake. The compass pivot point is now located somewhere along the perpendicular line.

Step 5. Experiment to get the desired arc or curve. Anchor a cord or rope at any chosen pivot point along the second string and attach a stake to the cord. Scribe an arc in the ground with the stake. Hold the cord taut. The closer the pivot point is located to the first string, the more curved the arc. The farther away the pivot point is located from the first string, the less curved the arc.

Step 6. Drive wooden stakes along the scribed curve as markers.

Making Curved Fences—Straight, short sections of fencing between closely spaced posts give a curved appearance.

Retaining walls can collapse from the weight of wet soil.

Wood construction projects that do not trap water will last longer than those that are unprotected and drained properly.

Posts sitting on paving should be elevated above the surface with post anchors. This allows water to drain away. Posts set in concrete collars should be in contact with gravel at the bottom. The gravel permits water to drain through and away. Slope collar tops to drain water away from posts. Posts with ends sealed in concrete will be sitting in a pool of water.

E

Epoxy—A strong, hard, resistant adhesive used in glues and coatings.

Epoxy Cement—A mixture of epoxy, sand and cement paste used as a patching compound. Mix epoxy cement just before use. Discard excess.

Espalier—Method of training and pruning plants. A plant trained and pruned to grow flat against a framework or wall. Espaliers save space and produce fruit or flowers without casting much shade. Apples and pears are traditional subjects for espaliers.

Evaporation—The process of changing a liquid or solid into vapor. Removal of moisture from anything by heating or drying.

Evapotranspiration—The total water loss from soil through the process of direct *evaporation* and *transpiration* from the surfaces of plants. See *evaporation* listing above and *transpiration* listing on page 153.

Expansion Joint—A break placed vertically in a long wall to absorb pressure and prevent buckling when walls expand and contract.

F

Face Course—Coursed layers of brick, block or stone on the wall face.

Fasteners—Various devices used to fasten or join objects together. Fasteners include nails, screws, metal anchors and ties, bolts and nuts, staples, turnbuckles, hinges and latches. Common connectors are described on page 154.

Fence—A protective barrier made from wood, metal or wire mesh. Fences are used as boundaries or for protection or confinement.

Fiberglass Panels—Fiberglass made of polyester reinforced with fibrous glass mesh. Fiberglass is available in various translucent colors. Fiberglass panels are cut to size by supplier.

Fill Soil—Soil that has been added or placed on a site or behind a retaining wall as *backfill*. Fill soil must be moistened and compacted in layers to avoid settling problems.

Finial—A decorative piece or *crowning ornament* made on a lathe or constructed of chamfered, rectangular pieces. Finials are used to cap fenceposts. Many styles can be purchased.

Footing—Enlarged lower portion of a foundation. Footings are required under walls, piers, columns or posts. Footings provide a stable base and distribute the weight of a structure over a larger area. They support and help prevent tilting of structures. Footings are placed underground. The most stable post footings are *concrete collars*.

Foundation—The base that supports a wall or structure. Foundations are usually constructed of concrete or masonry.

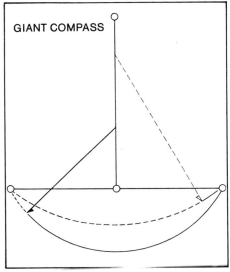

GIANT COMPASS

Giant compass is used to determine curves for long walls or fences. Method is described on page 148.

Making curved masonry walls requires adjusting mortar-joint distances. The outside edge of curved masonry walls should have mortar joints approximately 5/8 inch thick. The inside edge should have mortar joints approximately 1/8 inch thick.

Mark fencepost locations with stakes by measuring off the desired spacing around the arc. Set posts following the curve line.

Curved fences require curved stringers or rails. Use laminated *benderboards* or *kerfed* 1x4s. Benderboards are thin, narrow boards cut from plywood or laminated hardboard. Benderboards are easily bent. Benderboards are used to make curved forms for walls, landscape edging and sidewalks. See pages 118 and 119 for instructions on how to make kerfed boards.

Curved Masonry Walls—Curves in brick, concrete-block, adobe and glass-block walls are achieved by making the outside of the head mortar joints wider than the inside joints. Joint thickness for 8-inch units is approximately 1/8 inch thick on the inside and 5/8 inch thick on the outside.

Curved Timber Walls—Set poles, posts or railroad ties *upright* into wet concrete below grade. Dig a trench that extends below the frost line. Spread a 3-inch layer of gravel in the trench bottom. Loosely set posts and fill trench with concrete. Level posts vertically.

Curved Concrete Walls—Curves are made by constructing curved forms. Kerf plywood or board lumber to make forms. Use sheet metal nailed to numerous stakes to form tight curves. See the illustration on page 118.

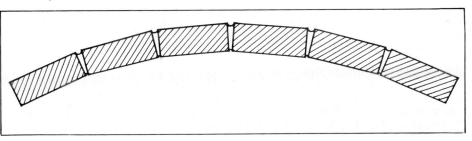

Frost Heaving—This refers to the movement of the soil and objects in it during cold weather. Frost heaving occurs as soil freezes and thaws. Fence and wall footings should be placed approximately 6 inches below the frost line. Concrete collars around fenceposts provide extra stability. See page 41.

Frost Line—The lowest level in soil that frosts or freezes. Soil does not shrink or swell below the frost-line depth in cold weather. The frost-line depth in the soil depends on winter temperatures, soil type and vegetation cover. Frost-line depth varies from 0 inches in warm-winter regions to about 2 feet in cold-winter areas. Consult local building departments about frost-line depth information in your region.

G

Gage—Refers to the different diameters of wire used in fencing or rods used in reinforcing bars. The smaller the gage number, the larger the wire diameter.

Galvanized—Refers to the process of dipping metal objects into a hot bath of metallic zinc. This process adds a zinc coating. The metallic-zinc coating retards rust. Nails, screws and metal connectors exposed to weather are often galvanized.

Gate—A movable framework or solid structure that swings on hinges. Gates control entrance or exit through an opening in a fence or wall.

Gate Stops—Gate stops keep a gate from swinging past the latch and weakening hinges. Gate stops can be made from a vertical strip of wood attached to the post. Gate stops can also be an extended piece of siding on either fence or gate.

Glass—A hard, brittle substance, usually transparent or translucent. Glass is made by heating or fusing silicates with soda or potash, lime and various metallic oxides. Textured glass provides privacy while permitting light to penetrate. Glass is the logical choice for structures where shade is not desired and light is welcomed.

Local building codes may specify tempered plate glass of minimum strength or require safety glass that has plastic or wire between two layers. Check building codes before you begin a project.

Glass is expensive and expert installation is recommended for this fragile material. Use stock-size panels to help reduce costs. Stock sizes are also cheaper to replace. Stock metal frames are worth consideration too. Mirror or solar reflective glass provides complete privacy by blocking views in and preserving views out.

Choose glass panels strong enough to resist strong wind. *Glass block* can be used for outdoor screens or walls too. It is more durable than glass panels. Transparent or translucent plastic can be used in place of glass.

Glass Block—A masonry unit made by fusing two formed pieces of pressed glass together. For curved or straight non-loadbearing walls and as panels or windows in other kinds of walls, glass block is unsurpassed in its elegance. Glass permits light to penetrate, but blocks wind. It is useful for small spaces and sunny exposures where conventional walls block light and cast too much shade.

Good-Neighbor Fence—A fence that has the same look on each side.

Grade—In lumber, grade refers to the appearance of the wood grain. Better, more-expensive grades of wood are clear and have no visible defects. See page 55.

In construction, grade refers to the ground level around a fence, wall or building. Grade can also refer to the degree of rise or descent of a sloping surface.

Grommets—These are large metal rings similar to large shoelace eyelets. They protect and reinforce holes in fabric. Grommets are placed in canvas or vinyl sheets to hold ropes or lacings. Grommet-setting tools are available from fabric stores or awning shops.

Grout—A thinned mortar-mix made by adding extra water to the mortar mixture. Grout is poured into masonry cavities—the space between brick wall wythes or concrete-block cells—to secure steel reinforcing or hardware and create a solid wall mass.

Grout Bag—A masonry tool consisting of a bag with a nozzle. Used for squeezing grout into mortar joints.

Guideline—See *mason's line*.

H

Head Joint—The mortar joint in a masonry wall running vertically between units.

Header Or Header Courses—A brick or building stone laid across the thickness of a wall. The short end of the brick is exposed in the wall face. A course or series of bricks laid across the thickness of a wall.

Heat Exchanger, Heat Reservoir—A device for transferring heat energy from a warmer medium to a cooler medium. Walls serve as heat exchangers by absorbing heat from the sun, storing heat in the masonry and radiating heat into the cooler air.

Hedges—A row of closely planted bushes, shrubs or trees that form a boundary or fence.

J

Joint—Place where two elements are joined. Joint type depends on design, construction technique and material. Masonry joints, see page 103. Woodworking joints, see page 44.

K

Kerf—A short, narrow, saw cut made across the width of plywood or board lumber. Kerf cuts across a board allow the board to bend. See *saw kerf*.

Key—A slot formed in concrete. A key locks the second pour of concrete to the first pour of concrete.

Keyed Footing—A concrete footing that contains a key to secure a wall. The wall is poured after the footing cures.

Kiln—A furnace or oven for drying lumber or baking bricks.

Kiln-Dried Lumber—Lumber dried in a kiln or large oven using heat. The process is used to dry lumber to a moisture content below that obtained in air-drying. The drying device is called a *dry kiln*.

L

Laid—See *lay*.

Latex Cement—A patching compound for making repairs to stucco or concrete walls. Latex cement is sold in bags containing a dry mixture of cement and latex. This mixture must be mixed with water. Liquid latex is also available in cans to mix with dry cement powder.

Lath—Thin, narrow strips of wood or metal used to build lattices. A framework for plaster or stucco, such as wire screening or expanded metal.

Lattice—Open structure of crossed

strips of wood or metal lath. Lattice is used as a screen or support structure for vines and shrubs.

Lay—To put down or place blocks, bricks, stones or other building units.

Lead—Stepped-back section of a wall that is built up at the ends and corners of walls first.

Level—A tool that indicates whether surfaces are horizontally level or vertically plumb. The leveling mechanism is a glass tube filled with fluid and an air bubble. The air bubble is centered and aligns with marks on the glass tube when the device is level.

Carpenter's levels are usually 2 feet long. *Mason's levels* make unit masonry jobs easier. They are 4 or 6 feet long. *Line levels* are small levels with hooks on each end. The hooks are attached over a line or string. The line level helps determine when the line is level.

Lime—A white substance, calcium oxide (CaO), obtained by the action of heat on limestone, shells and other materials containing calcium carbonate. Lime is used in making mortar and cement. When lime is hydrated, it can be used to neutralize acid soils.

Line Level—See *levels*.

Louver Fencing—This fence type has movable or fixed slats, called *louvers*, positioned at an angle. The louvers permit air circulation, light penetration or a view from one vantage point. Louver fences are useful for breeze control. The louvers can be positioned to block or admit prevailing wind or breezes.

Lumber—Refers to wood products available in standard dimensions and lengths. Includes stock sizes in different softwood species from cedar and pine to redwood. Available at lumberyards, home centers and building-supply outlets. See page 53.

M

Mason—A person who builds structures with masonry materials.

Masonry—The trade or art of building with masonry materials. The use of masonry materials. The structure that results from building with masonry materials such as bricks, concrete blocks and stones.

Mason's Level—A leveling device used by masons to determine whether a masonry wall is horizontally level and vertically plumb. Mason's levels are usually 4 or 6 feet long. See *levels*.

Mason's Line—String guideline used to align edges or level courses of masonry. Line is attached to a storyboard and raised to each course level.

Microclimate—Localized, small-scale variations in climate. They are influenced by topography, buildings and tree shelterbelts.

Walls, fences and screens can alter the microclimate in your yard by acting as windbreaks and creating shade. Masonry walls are effective heat reservoirs on the side facing the sun. Living fences of espaliers or hedges add moisture to air by evapotranspiration.

Miter—To cut at an angle. Two pieces are often mitered and joined together at a square corner.

Miter Box—A slotted tool for guiding a saw to cut miters.

Mortar—A mixture of cement, water and sand. Mortar contains no aggregates. Mortar preparation is an important step in the installation of masonry materials. Mortar consistency must be workable, but dry. If mortar is too wet, the masonry units will *float* or move out of place, causing uneven joints.

Mortar with the consistency of bread dough produces the best results. Commercial, premixed dry mortar will be adequate. Follow directions on the sack and prepare approximately one bucket of mortar at a time. A small amount will not dry and harden before it is used.

If you prefer, make your own mortar using a mixture of 1 part masonry cement and 3 parts sand. Add water until mortar is the proper consistency.

Mortise—A hole or slot cut in a fencepost to receive an element called a *tenon*.

N

Neat Cement—A mixture of cement and water. Neat cement contains no sand or aggregates.

Nominal Size—Refers to size of objects by name only. In masonry, describes the thickness and width of bricks or blocks after the addition of mortar joints. See pages 87 and 96 for nominal sizes of masonry materials.

In lumber, refers to the dimensions, or thickness and width, of a board before it has been dressed and planed. Actual finished sizes vary slightly depending on the wood species. See page 57 for nominal sizes of lumber.

Norman Brick—A brick with nominal dimensions of 2-2/3x4x12''.

O

On Center—Designation of spacing. Measured from the center of one object to the center of the next. Posts are usually positioned on center. Stapled on center *both ways* means fastened both horizontally and vertically with staples.

Opaque—Refers to materials that do not allow light to pass through. Not transparent or translucent.

P

Paint—See fence finishes, page 49.

Palings—See lumber, page 53.

Penta—See preserving wood, page 158.

Picket Fence—A fence made of upright pales, pickets or stakes.

Pilasters—A rectangular support or pier that projects from a wall surface. Pilasters function in the same manner as columns and provide lateral strength. Pilasters reinforce walls to help prevent tilting and resist wind loading. They usually contain rebar and are filled full of grout. Pilasters permit construction of high, thin walls and reduce the amount of steel reinforcing necessary.

Pilasters are made by laying bricks or blocks in various patterns depending on the bond pattern. See the illustrations on page 108. Manufactured concrete-block pilaster units, called *pilaster blocks*, require less masonry skill to install.

Many walls end with attractive pilasters that support gates. Pilasters also provide decorative relief to wall surfaces. Footings must be widened at pilaster locations. Space pilasters approximately 12 feet on center.

Pilasters can also be used for panel wall construction. Panel walls, with two exterior faces and a hollow space between them, must be designed by engineers. Pilasters are supported by footings or contain vertical rebars. Horizontal rebars reinforce and tie the panel sections to the pilasters.

Place, Pour—In masonry, refers to the act of putting concrete in position. Placing concrete is referred to as a *pour* or *pouring*.

Plane Or Planed—In woodworking, refers to the act of making the broad surfaces of a board flat, even or level.

Plastic Panels—Clear or translucent sheets of plastic made of acrylic. These sheets are available in various colors, textures and patterns. Colors may fade when exposed to sunlight over a period of time.

Plastic panels are lightweight and resist breakage. They have light transmission qualities similar to glass and are more economical.

Plastic panels may be cut with a fine-blade saw or portable sabre saw.

Plumb—Refers to straight up and down, or to make something exactly vertical. A weight attached to a cord.

Plumb Bob—A weight attached to a cord, sometimes called a *plumb*. A plumb bob is used as a guide to make a wall or fence vertical. A plumb bob is also used to locate reference points on the ground.

Plywood—Plywood is a panel made by laminating thin sheets of wood to a wood fiber core. The panels are coated with adhesives and pressed together under high temperatures and pressures. Plywood may have several layers. See page 55 for more detailed information on plywood grades for construction use.

Pointing—Troweling mortar into a joint after a masonry wall is laid.

Portland Cement—The original patent name given to cement in 1824 by its English inventor. Named because of its resemblance to limestone quarried on the Isle of Portland, Great Britain.

Portland cement is made by heating clay and crushed limestone to a *clinker*, a hard fused mass of stony matter. The clinker is ground to a fine, powdered state.

Post Anchors—Metal connectors that hold posts securely to walls or poured concrete. See *fasteners*. Post anchors slightly elevate the base of posts and are preferred for use on paving.

Pour—Refers to the act of placing concrete in a form.

Precut Lumber—Refers to lumber that has been precut to length at lumberyards, home centers or building material outlets. Precut lumber is usually available in 2-foot increments— 2-foot, 4-foot, 6-foot, 8-foot, 10-foot and 12-foot lengths.

Prepackaged Concrete Mixes—Commonly called *premix* concrete. Cement and aggregates, all premeasured, are thoroughly dried and mixed. These ingredients are placed in 90-pound bags. They usually require no further preparations except for the addition of water. Prepackaged concrete mixes are excellent for small jobs and repairs. Convenient and somewhat expensive.

One 90-pound bag makes enough to set one fencepost or approximately 2/3 cubic foot of concrete. This may be economical for small jobs. Bagged sand-gravel mixes are also available.

Preservatives—Includes all chemicals or combinations of chemicals used to protect wood against deterioration from decay, insects, fire, weathering, water and chemical action. See feature section on opposite page.

R

Rail Or Stringer—The horizontal piece between fenceposts. The rail is used to support fence siding.

Raked Joints—One of several styles of *tooled* mortar joints. Raked joints produce a wall surface with deep shadow lines. The mortar is recessed approximately 1/2 inch.

Raking joints on brick or block walls emphasizes individual units. Raking joints on stone walls can make the mortar appear to disappear, producing the look of a dry-laid wall. See page 103 for descriptions of different joints. See *strike*.

Random Rubble—A stone wall pattern using uncut stone laid in uneven or irregular courses.

Ready-Mix Concrete—This concrete is mixed at a concrete plant or in trucks on the way to the job. Ready-mix concrete is ready for placement.

Rebar—Abbreviation for *reinforcing bar*, sometimes called *rods*. Round, steel bars placed in concrete and unit masonry walls for reinforcement purposes. Sized in 1/8-inch increments. A No. 4 rebar is 1/2 inch in diameter.

Reinforcing, Reinforcing Bar—Concrete and unit masonry walls can support large stationary loads or compressive forces. They will not withstand strong lateral forces.

Steel rebar has great flexible strength to withstand lateral forces, but little compressive strength.

Concrete or unit masonry walls are reinforced with steel rebars and header courses. Use of rebar and header courses combines the complementary strengths of both materials.

Walls should be reinforced both horizontally and vertically. Footings are usually reinforced horizontally.

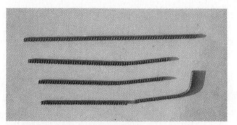

Reinforcing rod or rebar.

Vertical rods are connected to footing bars with steel ties. These steel ties strengthen the wall.

In most areas, particularly earthquake country, building codes specify minimum reinforcing requirements.

Retaining Wall—A wall used for holding back soil or other materials. Retaining walls may be constructed from masonry or wood materials.

Rods—See *rebar*.

Roman Brick—Brick with nominal dimensions of 2x4x12".

Rowlock—A row of brick headers laid on edge so ends are visible. Often used to cap a wall. See page 102.

Rubble—Rough stones or broken pieces of brick and concrete.

S

Saw Kerf—Short cuts made across the width of plywood or board lumber. Saw kerfs remove part of the bulk of the wood on one side and allow the board to be bent.

Make kerfs across the grain in board lumber. Use a power circular saw to cut about 2/3 of the way through the wood at equally spaced intervals. Soak lumber in water until it is pliable, then bend toward the kerfs.

Scratch Coat—A scored coat of mortar or stucco laid over 1-inch-mesh chicken wire or self-furring wire lath. The scratch coat provides a bonding surface for following coats of mortar or stucco on painted masonry, adobe, irregularly surfaced walls or stud walls. The scratch pattern is achieved with a stiff wire brush.

Screed—Process of striking off excess concrete to level and smooth top surface of walls or footings.

Screen Block—Concrete block made with open grille pattern. Blocks are laid on end in wall construction.

Sealer—See fence finishes, page 49.

Self-Furring Wire Lath—Wire material made for installing stucco.

Set—The point in time when concrete hardens or sets. Concrete cannot be worked after it has set.

Setting Time—The amount of time a cement remains *plastic* or workable. This time period should be long enough to allow placement of concrete without affecting finishing operations.

Single Placement, Single Pour—Installation of wet, fluid concrete that fills all formwork at one time. Low walls with simple footings are usually made in a single placement. High or long walls require several placements.

Slope—The degree of inclination of a hillside. Measured in inches of rise per horizontal foot.

Slump Stone, Slump Block—A concrete-block material that has a curved face surface. This curved surface gives walls of slump stone an appealing, irregular quality that looks similar to adobe.

Split Block—Concrete block made by cracking blocks in two pieces to produce a stonelike surface on the split face.

Spreader Forms—See forms, pages 75 and 118.

Square Footage—Calculated by multiplying the surface length times the height. Square footage is used to estimate the amount of materials needed for construction.

Stain—See fence finishes, page 49.

Stopboards—Boards set in formwork to hold wet concrete. Stopboards separate one pour from another pour during the construction of poured-concrete walls.

Stops—See gate stops, page 141.

Storyboard, Storypole—A long board marked at intervals corresponding to the height of each course of bricks or concrete blocks in a wall.

Stretcher—Brick or block unit laid in a horizontal course along the length of a wall. See pages 87, 88, 90 and 100.

Strike—A *gate strike* or *stop* prevents a gate from swinging past the latch and damaging the hinges. To *strike* or *tool* joints means to remove excess concrete and finish joints in a pattern. Striking must be done before joints *set*. Several different masonry tools are used for striking.

Strikeoff—To remove excess concrete from forms or joints.

Stringer—See *rail*.

Structural Brick—Hollow, oversize brick made to the same dimensions as concrete block and used in the same manner. Usually reinforced with steel and filled with grout.

Stucco—Plaster or cement used for surfacing inside or outside walls.

Stucco can have a smooth or rough texture. It is easy to paint.

Stud, Studs—Vertical supports, usually wooden 2x4s, that form walls. Surface coverings of plywood or drywall are attached to studs.

Subgrade—The gravel, rock or soil surface that concrete footings are built on. The subgrade is leveled and thoroughly tamped down or compacted to provide a firm base. Usually located below ground level.

T

Tamp—To compact soil or fill material with repeated light blows usng a *tamper*. A tamper is a flat tool that can be rented or homemade from lumber. Fill soil must be compacted to prevent settling. Concrete is tamped immediately after pouring to remove air pockets and distribute aggregate throughout the mixture.

Tenon—A cut element on a fence rail that fits into a *mortise*.

Tension Curves—Crimps in wire fencing to permit expansion and contraction with changing temperatures.

Terraces—Raised, flat mounds of earth with sloping sides. Terraces are usually a series of earthen platforms rising one above the other on a hillside. Retaining walls are used to hold earth in place.

Tie—Metal reinforcing unit used to join wythes or veneers to walls.

Toenail—To drive a nail at an angle through a wooden joint.

Tool—Compacting and shaping of mortar joints with a masonry tool. See *strike*.

Transit-Mix Concrete—See *ready-mix concrete*.

Translucent—Refers to being obscure, or semitransparent, as in frosted glass. Allows light to pass through, but vision is blocked.

Transparent—A clear material, such as glass, that allows light to pass through. Objects can be seen through transparent materials.

Transpiration—Process of giving off moisture.

Trowel—Any of several small hand tools used in masonry. Trowels are used for spreading, smoothing and scooping concrete and mortar.

Tuck Pointing—Filling in cut-out or defective mortar joints in masonry. Fresh mortar is applied to the joint with a trowel.

Turnbuckle—Fastener used to in-

crease or decrease tension on a wire. See page 139.

U

Undisturbed Soil—The original soil formed in place. The native soil. It is not fill soil. Many housing developments are actually built on fill soil.

Unit Masonry—Masonry of bricks, blocks or stone units as opposed to poured-concrete masonry.

Unstable Soils—Soils that have the potential to move. The most common causes of soil movement or *slumping* are expansion and contraction caused by freezing and thawing, gravity-induced movement on slopes or settling of improperly compacted fill soil.

Frost heaving of fenceposts or walls can be avoided by setting posts or footings deep enough to reach below the frost line.

Settling of fill can be avoided by watering the fill and compacting or tamping it.

Building terraces with retaining walls is an effective way to minimize soil movement on slopes.

Some clay soils are so unstable, especially if saturated with water, that little can be done to prevent slumping. If your soil is extremely unstable, consult an engineer before you attempt to build retaining walls.

V

Veneer—A thin masonry unit, usually a cut brick or stone, applied to the face of a concrete-block or poured-concrete wall. See page 92.

W

Wall—An upright structure of wood, stone or brick. Walls enclose, divide, support and protect.

Weather—Refers to the changes in color, texture or efficiency of wood or masonry materials by continued exposure to wind, rain, sun, frost, snow and other elements.

Weep Holes—Openings placed in mortar joints for drainage of water.

Wood Shrinkage—Refers to loss of volume in *green* or fresh-cut lumber. Usually occurs in wood that has not been kiln-dried.

Workability—The relative ease or difficulty of placing and working concrete in its final position in forms.

Wythe—The width of one course of common bricks.

Construction Fasteners

This is a sampling of the most useful fasteners for fence, wall and gate projects. Some fasteners perform only one special function. Others serve several functions. Nails in combination with metal connectors provide more strength and perform more jobs than nails used alone.

Always choose fasteners that resist corrosion and rust. Rust weakens a fastener's strength and causes stains on surfaces. Rust-resistant fasteners are aluminum, stainless steel, galvanized, brass, chrome or zinc-plated. Galvanized nails and connectors may stain over time but are suited to many jobs. Zinc plating is more permanent.

Select nail and screw lengths to penetrate at least 2/3 of the way into the second object. See the charts in this section for sizes of nails and screws.

NAILS

There are almost as many kinds of nails as there are projects that require them. Steel nails are the most common. Nails are also made of aluminum, stainless steel, copper, brass and bronze.

Aluminum, copper, brass, bronze and stainless-steel nails are rustproof. Steel nails will rust.

Kinds Of Nails—The kind of nail is determined by several factors. These include the nail head, shank shape and type of use. Nail heads are either finish or common. The finishing nail has a thin head that can be set below the surface. A common nail has a flat, round head that protrudes past the shank surface.

Nails are termed wire, box, casing, finishing and brad.

Wire Nails are usually called *common nails*. Wire nails have a broad head and shaft. They have a tendency to split wood. Common wire nails are used for rough, heavy construction work. *Duplex* or double-headed wire nails are used for temporary construction. Duplex nails are perfect for fastening bracing or for concrete form-work construction because they are easy to remove.

Box Nails are similar to common nails, but they have a thinner shaft and less tendency to split wood. Box nails are used for fine construction and assembly work.

Finishing Nails are for light construction and fine work. Heads may be countersunk below the surface and holes filled. Finishing nails are used for detailed cabinetry work.

Casing Nails are the same as finishing nails, but their heads are driven flush with surfaces, not countersunk. Casing nails are used for cabinet and trim work.

Brads are smaller and thinner than finishing nails. Use brads for finer work and small objects.

Nail Shanks—Shank shape, nail length and diameter determine the holding power of nails. The longer the nail and bigger the shank diameter, the greater the nail's holding power.

Smooth-Shank Nails have the least holding power.

Barbed Nails have horizontal or herringbone indentations on the shank. These ridges lock the nail to wood and hold better than smooth-shank nails. Use barbed nails for green wood or where great strength is desired.

Threaded Nails provide the best holding power. They may have *annular, spiral* or *knurled* shanks.

Annular-threaded nails, sometimes called *ring-shank* nails, give the greatest holding power.

Spiral-threaded nails, sometimes called *screw* or *drive nails,* turn into the wood when driven with a hammer. They have good holding power and are used for hardwoods.

Knurled-threaded nails, called *masonry nails,* have a vertical thread for driving into masonry units. Masonry nails are forged from case-hardened steel. They are available in several styles—round, square or fluted. Masonry nails are used to join wood studs, furring strips and 2x4 plates to masonry walls and paving.

Use a heavy ball-peen or hand-drilling hammer for driving masonry nails. Never use a regular hammer! Always wear safety goggles.

Nail Sizes—Nails come in many lengths and diameters. Nails are traditionally sized by the term *penny,* abbreviated *d.* This designation comes from the Latin word, *denarius,* or penny cost for 100 nails.

Originally, nails were sold by the number of nails per pound, called the *pennyweight* system. The system now refers to the length of the nail—a 2d nail is 1'' long, a 3d nail is 1-1/4'' long and a 16d nail is 3-1/2'' long. See the chart on page 155 for nail sizes.

SCREWS

Screws are threaded fasteners. Screws provide greater holding power than nails and screws can be reused. Screws are more expensive and time-consuming to install than nails. Holes must be predrilled to use screws.

Screws are used to attach hardware to wood or metal.

Kinds Of Screws—Screws are available in several types. The type of screw is determined by the use, the type of head and the size.

Screw Uses—There are two basic uses for screws. Screw use refers to the type of material it will be used in and the type of threads.

Wood screws are used for fastening to wood. They have a different type of thread than metal screws. *Sheet-metal screws* are used for fastening to metal. Threads on sheet-metal screws are deeper and at a flatter angle than wood screws.

Screw Heads—There are two basic screw heads. *Regular-head* screws have one slot in the top and are used with straight-blade screwdrivers. *Phillips-head* screws have two crossing slots in the top of the head instead of one slot. They are used with a Phillips screwdriver.

There are three basic screw-head shapes available with either a regular- or Phillips-head screw. *Flat-head screws* have a flat head and conical base. They are set flush with the surface or slightly below the surface. *Round-head screws* have a rounded head with a flat bottom surface. They protrude above the work surface. Round-head screws are used for temporary construction or in combination with washers for greater strength. *Oval-head screws* have a flatter, rounded head than round-head screws and a conical base.

Screw Sizes—Screws are available in different lengths and thread diameters.

Screw length is measured from the largest diameter of the bearing surface to the pointed end of the screw.

Screw diameter is measured on screws shorter than 1/4 inch in numbers from 0 to 10. Screws longer than 1/4 inch are measured in 1/16-inch increments up to 1/2 inch long. Screws longer than 1/2 inch are measured in 1/8-inch increments up to 2 inches long. Screws 2 inches long or longer are measured in 1/4-inch increments up to 3 inches long. Screws longer than 3 inches are special items.

Comparative Screw Sizes

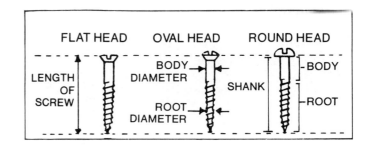

FLAT HEAD   OVAL HEAD   ROUND HEAD

LENGTH OF SCREW — BODY DIAMETER — ROOT DIAMETER — SHANK — BODY — ROOT

SCREW SIZE CHART

Length	\#0	\#1	\#2	\#3	\#4	\#5	\#6	\#7	\#8	\#9	\#10	\#11	\#12	\#14	\#16	\#18	\#20	\#24
1/4 inch	0	1	2	3														
3/8 inch			2	3	4	5	6	7										
1/2 inch			2	3	4	5	6	7	8									
5/8 inch				3	4	5	6	7	8	9	10							
3/4 inch					4	5	6	7	8	9	10	11						
7/8 inch							6	7	8	9	10	11	12					
1 inch							6	7	8	9	10	11	12	14				
1-1/4 inch								7	8	9	10	11	12	14	16			
1-1/2 inch							6	7	8	9	10	11	12	14	16	18		
1-3/4 inch									8	9	10	11	12	14	16	18	20	
2 inch									8	9	10	11	12	14	16	18	20	
2-1/4 inch										9	10	11	12	14	16	18	20	
2-1/2 inch													12	14	16	18	20	
2-3/4 inch														14	16	18	20	
3 inch															16	18	20	
3-1/2 inch																18	20	24
4 inch																18	20	24
	.060 / 0	.073 / 1	.086 / 2	.099 / 3	.112 / 4	.125 / 5	.138 / 6	.151 / 7	.164 / 8	.177 / 9	.190 / 10	.203 / 11	.216 / 12	.242 / 14	.268 / 16	.294 / 18	.320 / 20	.372 / 24

SCREW BODY DIAMETER (in inches) AND SHANK NUMBER EQUIVALENT

Comparative Nail Sizes

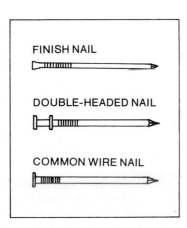

FINISH NAIL

DOUBLE-HEADED NAIL

COMMON WIRE NAIL

COMMON WIRE NAIL SIZE CHART

Size	Length Inches	Gage Number	Approximate Number to Pound
60d	6	2	11
50d	5-1/2	3	14
40d	5	4	18
30d	4-1/2	5	24
20d	4	6	31
16d	3-1/2	7	49
12d	3-1/4	8	63
10d	3	9	69
9d	2-3/4	10-1/4	96
8d	2-1/2	10-1/4	106
7d	2-1/4	11-1/2	161
6d	2	11-1/2	181
5d	1-3/4	12-1/2	271
4d	1-1/2	12-1/2	316
3d	1-1/4	14	568
2d	1	15	876

SCREW EYES

Screw eyes have one threaded end to fasten to wood. The other end is bent into an eye-shape. J-shaped hooks may also be formed on one end. Screw eyes are used for attaching wire to wood, often in combination with turnbuckles.

SCREW ANCHORS

Screw-in anchors are all-purpose fasteners. They can be used in hollow and solid walls and in almost all materials, from wood to concrete. There are several different types.

Plastic Anchors—These are used for mounting small items on walls. A hole is drilled in the wall and the plastic anchor is driven in with a hammer. The screw is screwed in the anchor and the plastic expands against the inside of the hole.

Nylon Expansion Anchors—They work in basically the same way as plastic anchors.

Nylon Drive Anchors—These anchors use a nail instead of a screw. As the nail is driven into the anchor, the plastic expands against the inside of the hole.

HOLLOW WALL FASTENERS

Two types of fasteners are used for hollow walls.

Toggle Fasteners—They work on a spring principle. The holding arms open after the bolt and holder are inserted into the hole. The arms grip the wall as the bolt is tightened. Bolts are selected according to the thickness of the wall. Lengths range from 2 to 8 inches and diameters from 1/8 to 5/16 inch thick.

Metal Expansion Anchors—Also called *molly bolts,* these anchors have a bolt or screw in a metal sleeve. The sleeve is placed in the hole and the screw is turned. The sleeve expands against the wall from the inside. The sleeve locks in place and the screw can be removed and replaced.

BOLTS

Bolts are used for heavy-duty fastening jobs in combination with nuts and washers. Bolts are threaded rods. They are stronger than screws. Holes are predrilled and the bolt is inserted. A nut is threaded on the bolt and tightened with a wrench.

Anchor Bolts Or J-Bolts—These fasteners are set into wet concrete, grout or mortar to hold wooden elements.

Lag Bolts Or Lag Screws—These types of fasteners are easier to drive than screws of the same size because of the bolt heads. Lag screws are used where it is not practical to use a bolt and nut. Apply wax to the screw end if it is difficult to drive.

Carriage Bolts—Used with a nut to attach posts to anchors or to substitute for J-bolts. Carriage bolts are versatile and can be used for many jobs. The square shoulder holds the bolt as the nut is tightened. Use a washer on the nut for greater strength.

Eye Bolt—This bolt is the same as a screw eye, but it is larger, sturdier and attached by a threaded bolt and nut. Eye bolts are used for fastening wires, often by combining them with turnbuckles.

Expansion Bolt—Commonly called a *masonry bolt and anchor.* This bolt is used to fasten objects to masonry joints or walls. Predrill the hole in masonry with a power drill and carbide-tip drill. Insert the expansion bolt and shield in the hole. A lead shield around the shaft expands and grips the inside of the hole as the bolt head is turned.

METAL CONNECTORS AND ANCHORS

These fasteners are often used in combination with other fasteners. They provide more strength and perform more jobs than nails, screws or bolts used alone. All metal connectors are available in flat black or galvanized. They can be painted any color.

Metal connectors are sized for rough or surfaced lumber. Some connectors have metal prongs. These sharp prongs hold connectors in place before nailing. These are particularly useful for fences, gates and walls.

Post Anchor—Sometimes called a *post base anchor.* These fasteners anchor posts to concrete paving, wooden decking or to poured-concrete walltops. Many shapes are available. Some of these anchors can be set into mortar joints of masonry walls. Post anchors can elevate posts above ground. This makes them useful in areas with standing water. Use an ex-

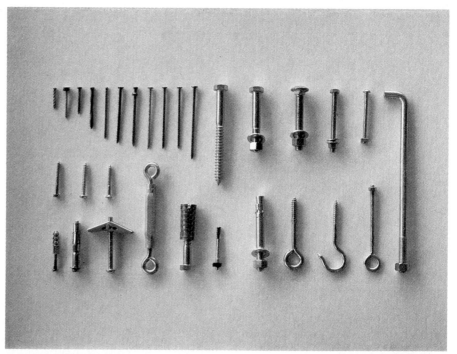

This photograph shows some of the common fasteners used in fence, gate and wall construction. Top row, left to right: Screw nail, aluminum twist nail with neoprene washer (used for corrugated fiberglass panels), joist-hanger nail (used for metal connectors), masonry nail, 10d finish nail, 16d vinyl-coated sinker, duplex nail, 16d galvanized box nail, 16d common nail, 16d box nail, 20d spike, lag screw, machine bolt, carriage bolt, full-thread machine bolt, stove bolt and J-shape anchor bolt (far right). Center row, left to right: Round-head wood screw, oval-head wood screw and flat-head wood screw. Bottom row, left to right: Plastic anchor with screw, molly bolt, toggle bolt, turnbuckle, lead expansion anchor with lag screw, 'red-head' stud anchor, stud anchor, eye screw, screw hook and eye bolt.

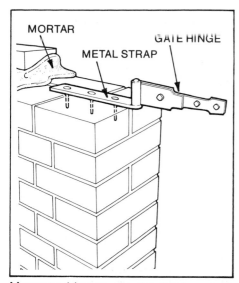

Masonry hinges are the best way to hang a gate from a brick or block wall. Metal strap hinges are placed in mortar joints as wall is built.

Post cap on left is used to attach beams or top rails to fenceposts. The anchor in the middle is attached to existing paving, decking or wall tops with an expansion bolt. Post anchors at right secure posts to masonry or decking. Anchor on the right is set into wet concrete. This anchor elevates the post base for drainage. Posts are bolted to anchors. Metal anchors may be painted.

pansion bolt to fasten post anchors to existing concrete. Use nails or bolts to attach post anchors to decking.

Fence Brackets—These brackets are especially useful for removable fence panels. Fence brackets are usually U-shape. They are sized for 1x4, 1x6, 2x3 or 2x4 lumber. The brackets are attached to the fenceposts and rails are dropped in between the posts. Fence brackets fill the space created by irregular rail lengths. They eliminate the need for blocking, toenailing or notching. Fence brackets can be used to fasten precut fencing rails or for positioning rails on posts to hold louvers at an angle.

Corner Braces—These fasteners give extra support to loadbearing joints at corners and joints.

L- And T-Straps—Metal connectors that are used individually or in pairs to eliminate toenailing. They make a strong connection between large-size members.

Post Caps—Post caps come in several styles. They are used to join large-size members. Post caps are helpful for butt connections.

Head Hangers—Use these fasteners for framing in stud walls.

Mud Sill Anchors—These anchors are used for connecting stud wall sill plates to wet concrete or masonry joints. The anchors are nailed to the sill and then set into wet concrete or mortar.

Turnbuckles—Use turnbuckles to tighten wire for gate bracing or in post-and-wire espalier fencing. Turning

the sleeve increases or decreases tension on wire. Turnbuckles are often available as part of *anti-sag* gate kits. These kits include corner brackets, cable clamps, wire cable and turnbuckles.

Masonry Ties—Ties are used to hold two wythes of masonry together. Some ties are used for holding veneer facing to walls. Ties can be inserted between mortar joints or courses. Ties can also be bolted into existing walls to secure veneer.

Z-Ties Or Z-Bars—This is a typical shape for steel masonry ties. This type is used for holding two wythes of masonry together.

Staples—Staples are U-shape with sharp points. Staples are used for fastening wire to wood. *Insulated* staples safely secure electrical wires to wooden fenceposts.

Special Anchors—Many different anchors are available or can be custom-made. They are used for setting into wet concrete or mortar joints to hold benches to walls or other construction jobs. If special anchors are out of your budget, experiment with readily available connectors. A good example is to use a post cap to support 4x4 cross members for a bench.

Latches—See page 134.
Hinges—See page 136.

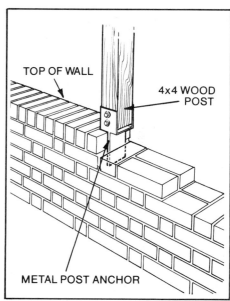

Metal post anchor is used to attach wooden posts to masonry walls or pilings. Anchor should be set in mortar joint while mortar is still wet. Allow mortar to cure before attaching posts to anchor.

Preserving Wood

Wood is a versatile and durable building material for outdoor structures such as fences and walls. Wood is also subject to decay. Decay is the result of wood-rotting fungi attacking and destroying wood.

Decay can be delayed by the application of one of several different chemical preservatives to protect the wood. These chemicals may be brushed or rolled on. Wood pieces may also be soaked in these chemicals or the chemical may be forced in the wood under pressure. This last process is called *pressure treating.*

CHEMICAL PRESERVATIVES

There are two basic types of preservatives. Oil-borne preservatives are introduced into wood in a solution of oil. Water-borne preservatives are introduced into wood in the form of a solution in water. Some common preservative chemicals are:

ACA—Ammoniacal copper arsenite. This preservative is a waterborne salt. Application of ACA results in wood with color ranging from natural to light green. Wood treated with ACA can be easily stained or painted.

ACC—Acid copper chromate. Another waterborne salt preservative. Same results as ACA.

CCA—Chromated copper arsenate. Same results as ACA.

PENTA—Pentachlorophenol dissolved in a hydrocarbon solvent. Pentachlorophenol is used on lumber that normally won't be stained or painted. It can also be used as a primer before painting or staining. Penta is toxic to plants and people.

CREOSOTE—Tar distillate. Creosote is a black, smelly preservative that is oily and virtually impossible to paint or stain.

Naturally decay-resistant wood species—redwood, red cedar, cypress and locust—must be treated with chemical preservatives if they will be in contact with soil. If these woods are treated with preservatives, they can last longer than ten years.

Use care in handling chemical preservatives. Wear rubber gloves and safety goggles to protect your hands and eyes.

Pressure-Treated Lumber—Penta or water-borne salts are forced into the cells of wood under extreme pressure. The chemicals are *locked in* the wood. The treatment is clean and dry, and

Pressure-treated timbers in low retaining wall are weathered to a natural gray.

treated lumber is generally safe for human and animal contact.

Pressure-treated lumber lasts 50 years or more, even in contact with moisture. Several chemicals are used for pressure treatment. Choose double-digit types if the lumber contacts soil or water.

LP-2 And LP-22 Lumber is treated with waterborne salts. The wood typically has a greenish color and a clean, dry surface.

LP-3 And LP-33 Lumber is treated with penta in light hydrocarbon solvents. The wood usually has a light-brown color. Additional steam treatment gives the wood a clean, dry surface. Avoid LP-3 or LP-33 treated woods with an oily surface.

LP-4 And LP-44 Lumber is treated with penta in liquified petroleum gas or methylene chloride. These woods

have no color change and a clean, dry surface.

LP-5, LP-55, LP-7 And LP-77 Lumber should be avoided. LP-5 and LP-55 are commonly known as creosote. LP-7 and LP-77 lumber is treated with penta in an oily solvent.

FINISHING TREATED LUMBER

Most woods treated with preservatives may be painted or stained. The exceptions are treated woods with oily surfaces. Surfaces should be clean, dry and primed. If left unpainted, pressure-treated wood weathers to an attractive silver-gray color similar to that of untreated wood. Pressure-treated wood will not take on the black stain markings characteristic of old, weathered redwood. These stains are caused by fungus.

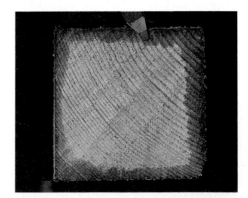

Above: Brush additional preservative on cut ends of treated and pressure-treated lumber.

Left: Applying preservatives to large timbers is not difficult. Make a trough to hold preservative and place timbers in trough.

INDEX

5.72709153867